SO-ASI-785

A Federal Resume Writing Workbook

FROM THE AUTHOR OF THE FEDERAL RESUME GUIDEBOOK

Reinvention Federal Resumes

Your Transition into the Future Federal Workforce

KATHRYN K. TROUTMAN

Reinvention Federal Resumes™
Your Transition into the Future Federal Workforce

Copyright 1997 by Kathryn Kraemer Troutman

ISBN: 0-9647025-1-7

Library of Congress Catalog Card Number:

Printed in the United States of America

All rights reserved. No part of this book may be reproduced in any form or by any means, or stored in a database or retrieval system, without prior permission of the publisher except in case of brief quotations embodied in articles or reviews. Making copies of any part of this book for any purpose other than your own personal use is in violation of United States copyright laws.

We have been careful to provide accurate information throughout this book, but it is possible that errors and omissions have been introduced. Please consider this in making any career plans or other important decisions. Trust your own judgment above all else and in all things.

The sample federal resumes used in this workbook are strictly fictitious, including reference names, titles, telephone numbers and social security numbers.

Published by:

The Resume Place, Inc.
310 Frederick Road
Baltimore, MD 21228
Phone: (410) 744-4324
Fax: (410) 744-0112
E-mail: Resume@ari.net

Author:	Kathryn Kraemer Troutman
Editor:	Bonita Kraemer and Bonny Kraemer Day
Book Design:	Bonny Kraemer Day, The Resume Place, Inc.
Cover Design:	Teal Carey, Cary Creative Design, Baltimore, MD (410) 744-8458

Acknowledgements

I would like to thank those who helped me create this resume writing workbook/training program: my workshop participants who were my first "in-class" resume writers, who taught me how to teach this challenging subject; and to those who helped me manage my resume writing business while I was researching the federal resume writing process.

I'd like to thank my contact at the Office of Personnel Management, who spoke to me frequently about the new Federal Resume program being introduced throughout government; Faith Williamson, government entrepreneur and Director, Career Management Center, Dept. of Health and Human Services, who managed the first popular "fee for service" Federal Resume writing program in government; and the Women's Executive Leadership program participants, who did a wonderful job writing their own Federal Resumes from my first training program.

Finally, I'd like to thank my sister, Bonny Day, book editor, designer and General Manager of The Resume Place, for her organizational assistance, design and formatting, and most importantly, patience in helping me produce this book while taking care of our resume clients in both offices. Without her help in all aspects of publishing, training, and resume writing, I would not be writing books now.

Kathryn K. Troutman,
President

Bonny Day,
General Manager

310 Frederick Road
Catonsville, MD 21228
(410) 744-4324
Fax: (410) 744-0112
e-mail: resume@ari.net

1725 K Street, NW
Washington, DC 20006
(202) RES-UMES (737-8637)
Fax: (202) 872-9217

The Resume Place, Inc.

Designer of the Federal Resume • Established in 1971

Dear Federal Resume Writers and Trainers,

Federal resumes are the key to entry and advancement in the federal workforce. Since the Office of Personnel Management consigned the SF-171 to the dumpster (along with the rest of the Federal Personnel Manual) agencies have been grappling with newer, more flexible, means of enabling applicants for positions to present their qualifications. This book will help you ride the emerging tide of best practices in writing your resume for the federal workforce.

Only three years ago -- in June of 1994 -- OPM declared the SF-171 a dinosaur and decreed that it should sink into the tar pits of history effective January 1, 1995. In adapting its application process to the information age, the Department of Defense -- still the largest civilian employer -- has expressed a strong preference for scannable resumes and has announced that it will reject documents longer than three pages. So much for voluminous 171s assembled in black, 3-ring binders. What you can't get on three pages, won't be scanned. These are the new rules. This book will help you win in the new job hunting environment.

The Department of Defense has initiated a process that will have echo effects in every federal agency. As Dick Whitford, OPM's Director of Employment Information Services, told Government Executive magazine, "Now that we have eliminated the SF-171, the whole thrust is on an applicant's describing his or her specific background -- his or her knowledge, education, experiences, and skills -- in a way that is germane to the specific job he or she is applying for." Tom Kell's article, "The Paper Dinosaur," Government Executive magazine (September, 1997) describes the challenges of change in this starting block of federal hiring.

My own experience with writing applications for federal employment exceeds 25 years. I developed an expanded form for the SF-171 a generation ago, but I also sustained an active clientele of private sector applicants. In many cases, I assisted federal employees who were venturing into the private sector in transforming their "life-history 171" into the briefer resumes that are routinely used by most private employers. When OPM tossed the SF-171 into the dumpster, I published The Federal Resume Guidebook to introduce federal employees to the new format. In addition, during the past three years I have conducted hundreds of hours of seminars for federal employees to assist their efforts through the downsizing and transitions affecting many federal agencies.

Professional Resume Writing for Government and Private Industry

RP Website Developers:
Custom Websites for Business and Individuals

Resume Book Authors:
The Federal Resume Guidebook & PC Disk

The Federal Resume Writing Workbook, *Your Transition into the Future Federal Workforce*

The High School Student's Resume Writing Workbook, *Career Prep and Tech Prep Versions*

Resume Writing Training Programs

Internet:
www.resume-place.com/jobs
Rated *excellent* by Margaret Riley, The Riley Guide

This publication takes federal resumes in the real world of reinvented government. It presents a detailed focus on presenting your skills, accomplishments, and results in the language of the developing federal workplace. I have incorporated at many points the language of the National Performance Review's *Blair House Papers* – the little red book of reinventing government and presented them as Reinvention Resume Writing Tips throughout the workbook.

This workbook reflects what I have learned from teaching others to write federal resumes. In organizing my classes, I discovered that the section-by-section approach provided the easiest way to transform the SF-171 into a correct federal resume. I invited hundreds of students from my classes at the U.S. Department of Agriculture Graduate School and in the Women's Executive Leadership Program to submit samples of their efforts at writing federal resumes to me. I have benefited enormously from their creative approaches to presenting their careers, and they have written back to express their thanks for the suggestions and modifications that I have recommended to their federal resumes. This workbook will enable you to take the best from all of our efforts.

I have also added a chapter to the book to reflect the Department of Defense's use of Resumix™, a scanning technology for screening resumes for its agency and regional offices. "Writing a Scannable Resume" details the requirements to get your resume included in the resume database that will support DOD. Note: If the resume is longer than three pages, they stop scanning. The Resumix™ database does not provide for KSAs, so it is especially important to get your resume into a format that presents your vital skills up front. I have included the DOD websites in the Appendix of this workbook.

The best federal resume will present you in your most attractive light. In presenting your qualifications in their best light, it always helps to focus on the skills and background that employers want and need. This workbook emphasizes orienting your federal resume toward the skills and qualifications that federal employers seek when they announce position vacancies. I have included a detailed analysis of a vacancy announcement and "before" and "after" samples of a resume for a competitor for the position. This workbook provides everything that you need to present your qualifications in a manner best suited to the job opportunity that attracts you.

Thanks for allowing me to assist your first steps on this road to your next job.

Best wishes,

Kathryn K. Troutman

Table of Contents

CHAPTER 3. ANALYZING AN ANNOUNCEMENT

CHAPTER 4. MODIFYING YOUR RESUME

CHAPTER 5. WRITING A SCANNABLE FEDERAL RESUME

CHAPTER 6. TRANSITION RESUMES to the PRIVATE SECTOR

APPENDIX

Reinvention Resume Writing Tips

Reinventing government means something to everyone in government.

➢ Every <u>supervisor</u> needs to get power to the front lines and raise the spirit of the workforce.
➢ Every <u>service provider</u> needs to put customers first.
➢ Every <u>regulator</u> needs to use the leverage available through partnerships.
➢ Everyone in government needs to know the rules of the road to reinvention, because we need everyone's push to propel us down the road fast enough.

Vice President Al Gore, The Blair House Papers
National Performance Review, 1997

Vice President Gore says that the single biggest challenge facing reinvention is helping agency leaders/employees implement the principles of The Blair House Papers in the everyday workings of their organizations.

Pat Wood, Reinvention Express, June 6, 1997

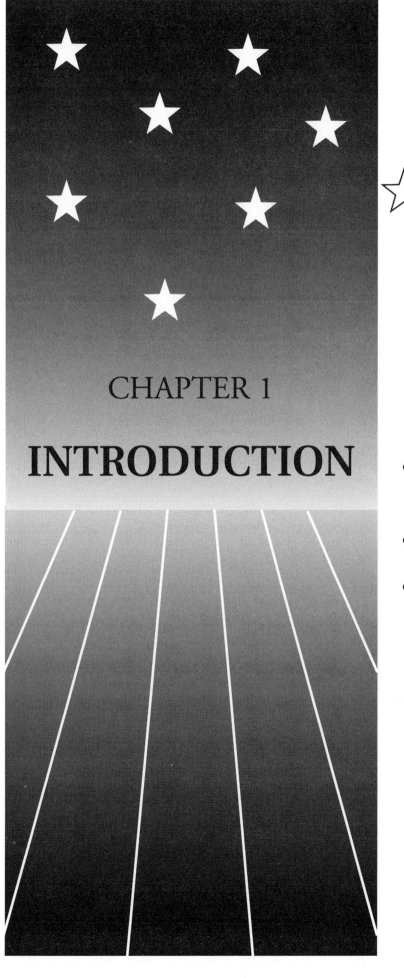

CHAPTER 1

INTRODUCTION

- Why are you writing a resume?

- Resume is a Marketing Tool

- A Targeted Approach

Introduction to
Targeted Resume Writing

Why are you using this workbook to apply for a new job?

Simple question. Let's try some complicated answers. Options include:

(1)   I feel I have reached a dead end in my federal career, and I want a resume that will help me get a new federal job in a better field.

(2)   I have had three calls from other agencies wanting to see my resume, and I need to think about how to comply with federal resume requirements.

(3)   I have had three promotions in the past five years, and I know that an SES option is in the works. I need to put together the most impressive document that I can.

(4)   I am three years away from retirement but facing a RIF. I need help to hang on in the federal sector.

(5)   I have had enough of budget cuts and RIFs. I need something to get me on the road to a good private sector job.

What? None of these are your answers? Not surprising. Everyone has an individual answer, but that question will affect everything that you do with a resume.

In writing this workbook, we want you to be able to approach the task of writing your federal resume exactly the way that a professional resume writer would do it. That means starting with setting an objective -- that is in terms of the position that you want -- then organizing the resume to present your qualifications for it in the most effective way.

For this reason, we include a detailed review of a sample federal job advertisement, analysis of what the advertising agency is seeking, then go through one applicant's best attempt at a resume and rewrite it to focus on what the agency says that it wants to see.

A resume is ...

A marketing tool. It is the first vehicle that you have to present yourself to an anonymous person -- very often to a review panel convened by a personnel specialist -- and to get acquainted.

An exceptional resume can move you from the "qualified" to the "best qualified" candidate category. It makes the difference between getting an interview and getting a letter that ends: "We regret to inform you that another candidate has been selected for the position. Thank you for letting us consider your application, and best wishes for your future career."

Even an outstanding resume will not stand alone in landing you a position. Each competitive position will involve an interview, and -- especially if you are changing agencies -- the resume will be the only information that the selecting official has as your background when you appear for the interview. The interviewer might devote five minutes to the resume in preparation for the interview. *These few pieces of paper will form the first impression that your interviewer gets.* First impressions can open the door to favorable lasting positions if the resume is well constructed.

A federal resume is . . .

A replacement for the SF-171 and the OF-612. Unlike the SF-171 that was rigid in format and organization, the federal resume can be organized to present your best skills and accomplishments on page one if you wish. Also, the new federal resume can be designed to be a "job-related" document instead of the previous "life history."

Reduction in force in government means serious competition

The Federal Workforce Restructuring Act of 1994 committed federal agencies to reduce the federal workforce by 272,900 positions by 1999. Most of those cuts have already been made. The federal workforce is far from stable, but even at its reduced size -- 1.8 million civilian employees -- federal personnel officials plan on a six percent turnover rate each year. In a Cabinet Department of 100,000 employees, that means 6,000 people will retire, quit, die, or be fired, and 6,000 people will be hired to replace them.

Within that 1.8 million person workforce, that computes into 108,000 hires each year. Even the Department of Defense -- which has eliminated 288,000 positions since 1989 -- still leads federal agencies in annual hiring. The opportunities are there, but a federal resume provides you a better medium to show the abilities that are increasingly attractive to the new federal hiring environment.

A career transition resume must be targeted to the announcement

This workbook studies an FAA job announcement line-by-line and analyzes one applicant's resume and critical skills. We have re-written and re-packaged this federal resume specifically to target this position. We realize that you will not re-write every federal resume for every announcement, but that you will re-draft the profile and accomplishments section at least with each application. We believe that by using the key words and phrases from the announcement, you will be much more likely to present your credentials in terms of the hiring official's needs. This will make you more likely to be seriously considered for the position.

GS-12 candidate seeking a GS-13 position

This candidate is currently a GS-12, Public Affairs Specialist with FAA. She is applying for a specialized position, International Aviation Operations Specialist, a GS-13/14. She must show expertise and ability to advance to senior level management, as well as describe as much specialized knowledge of International Aviation as possible. By highlighting the accomplishments on page one, we were able to combine on one-half page her best qualifications for the position.

Trust, But Verify

Our revision of "Roberta Spencer's" resume took elaborate license with any skills that a real applicant might have had. We had the freedom to create a career to illustrate different options in a resume. Your own resume, of course, cannot be creative in the same way. Remember, the resume is only a first impression, but it must send all the right signals. Actual job decisions will seldom, if ever, be made on the basis of the resume. Therefore, your resume needs to be supported by references, former supervisors, or anyone else who might be asked about it. Above all, you should be able to describe any claims on the resume to an interviewer on whom you want to make a favorable hiring decision. Your resume should make *you* comfortable discussing your career. An effective presentation is your first step on the road to selling yourself in today's federal job market.

Reinvention Resume Writing Tips

OUR REINVENTION MARCHING ORDERS INCLUDE:

➢ **Deliver great service** – treat the public the way top companies treat their customers.

➢ **Foster partnership and community solutions** – businesses have proven effective partners in achieving cleaner environment, worker safety and other regulatory compliance goals.

➢ **Reinvent to get the job done** - unlock the enormous, unused, human potential of the federal workforce. There should be a shift of resources from headquarters to the front lines, and capitalization on the positive power of competition.

Vice President Al Gore, The Blair House Papers
National Performance Review

CHAPTER 2

WRITING YOUR FEDERAL RESUME

- OF-510

- 12 Resume Writing Exercises

- The Basic Facts

- Work Experience

- Resume Focusing
  Techniques

- Putting It All Together

Getting Started

Getting started is one of the most difficult parts of resume writing. However, dividing the resume into components will make the process easier. Our exercises are designed to change your thinking from the former "life history" writing style to job-related writing style. We realize this is a challenge and very difficult for most federal employees. The overriding goal of this workbook is to assist you with writing a stand-out, interesting and personalized resume which presents you as an individual who can contribute to a new organization or position. Our experience with this workbook shows that 100% of those who read and follow our ideas will succeed in writing a great resume that is targeted toward their announcement. Let's review the 5 Ws and one H of your career and get ready to write now.

What Have You Done?

Your career provides the variety of experiences that will be essential to your next position. As any reporter or investigator learns quickly, there are six critical questions to be answered with any position -- **the five Ws and one H.**

Who Did I Work For?

Collect the background information from each job experience. The federal resume requires names and phone numbers of supervisors, agency names, the organization within the agency, address (at least city, state and zip code), starting and ending salaries (or GS series and ratings). If you have all of this information on your SF-171, you will have what you need. If not, you must assemble this information -- any omission of these elements can lead to rejection of your resume.

Where Was The Job?

The primary location of the position -- where was the office? -- needs to be identified with each position. If your position involved a great deal of travel (more than one week per month) and the position that you are seeking requires travel, this element should be included in the description. As will be shown through examples, the mention of travel does not need to be extensive or exhausting, but it should convey the experience and willingness that the employer is seeking.

When Did I Do It?

The federal resume also requires dates of employment for at least the past ten years. The month and year associated with each position are the minimum information required. In nearly all cases, job experiences (or other important qualifications) should be presented in reverse chronological order. The most recent experience (the highest degree, most recent professional training, etc.) should be first, with older or less significant education or training following, each in its own section.

This rule need not be followed mechanically. There are some unique situations where it is advantageous to present relevant skills in a functional order rather than chronologically. However, anyone using a functional presentation should remember the first question that occurs to a personnel specialist screening the application: What is the applicant trying to evade?

What Did I Do?

Don't be fooled. This is a very tricky question. Too many federal employees -- living with the memory of the SF-171 -- believe that people screening resumes need to know everything about the applicant's background. They fear that omission of the slightest detail will provide an advantage to other applicants.

Nothing could be more deadly than a resume that spends too much time copying every function listed in a position description. What is most important to get across on your resume is the information that makes your qualifications different from everyone else's. Every budget analyst compiles budget justifications at some point in a career. Every air traffic controller has to understand what instrument flight rules are. Every secretary types to qualify for the position. These are the starting points of a career. The critical skills are the ones that will be needed for the next job.

Effective presentations should attempt to describe your role in making a difference in the organization's results. "Wrote budget justifications to support a $300 million computer systems acquisition," says a bit more than the initial version of saying you compiled budget justifications. "Developed and presented budget justification that secured a $300 million appropriation for computer systems acquisition," adds a bit more.

Why Did I Do It?

Introductory economics texts will tell you that there is one reason for all human action -- money. In truth, people are willing to pay money because they have a reason to want a good service, some knowledge, skill, commitment to the public interest, or a host of other factors, and money is the easiest method of reducing those other interests to understandable terms. Even if your work is considered an unenviable chore that no one else would want to do, it contributes in some way to the mission of the agency. As federal agencies implement the Government Performance and Results Act of 1993, they will become increasingly aware of the ways in which each position contributes to the agency's mission. These links of position duties to agency missions should surface in vacancy announcements.

How Did I Do It?

This is the element that can be most important in conveying to evaluators your knowledge of the ***procedures*** to get the job done. Every employee provides some reports of his or her actions and accomplishments, but everyone knows that some presentations of material are better than others. Organizing information is most effective when presented in an order that the evaluator recognizes and that bears resemblance to the sequence in which the work is performed. Job blocks on a federal resume do not need to contain every detail of each position, but they do need to convey a sense of professional growth and accomplishment for most favorable consideration.

 **United States
Office of
Personnel
Management**

OF 510
(September 1994)

OPM'S Guidelines, "Applying for a Federal Job," OF-510

Here's what your resume or application must contain
(in addition to specific information requested in the job vacancy announcement)

JOB INFORMATION

❑ Announcement number, and title and grade(s) of the job for which you are applying

PERSONAL INFORMATION

❑ Full name, mailing address *(with ZIP Code)* and day and evening phone numbers *(with area code)*
❑ Social Security Number
❑ Country of citizenship *(Most Federal jobs require United States citizenship.)*
❑ Veterans' preference *(See reverse.)*
❑ Reinstatement eligibility *(If requested, attach SF 50 proof of your career or career-conditional status.)*
❑ Highest Federal civilian grade held *(Also give job series and dates held.)*

EDUCATION

❑ High school
    Name, city, and State *(ZIP Code if known)*
    Date of diploma or GED
❑ Colleges and universities
    Name, city, and State *(ZIP Code if known)*
    Majors
    Type and year of any degrees received
    (If no degree, show total credits earned and indicate whether semester or quarter hours.)
❑ Send a copy of your college transcript only if the job vacancy announcement requests it.

WORK EXPERIENCE

❑ Give the following information for your paid and nonpaid work experience related to the job for which you are applying. *(Do not send job descriptions.)*
    Job title *(include series and grade if Federal job)*
    Duties and accomplishments
    Employer's name and address
    Supervisor's name and phone number
    Starting and ending dates *(month and year)*
    Hours per week
    Salary
❑ Indicate if we may contact your current supervisor.

OTHER QUALIFICATIONS

❑ **Job-related** training courses *(title and year)*
❑ **Job-related** skills, for example, other languages, computer software/hardware, tools, machinery, typing speed
❑ **Job-related** certificates and licenses *(current only)*
❑ **Job-related** honors, awards, and special accomplishments, for example, publica–tions, memberships in professional or honor societies, leadership activities, public speaking, and performance awards *(Give dates but do not send documents unless requested.)*

> **THE FEDERAL GOVERNMENT IS
> AN EQUAL OPPORTUNITY EMPLOYER**

Federal Resume Writing Exercises

Section 1 - Who, When, Where?

THE BASIC FACTS
OF-510 Requirements

1. Job Information & Personal Data
2. Education
3. Training
4. Other Qualifications
5. Work Experience Outline

Section 2 - What?

WRITING YOUR JOB DESCRIPTIONS
Selling Yourself!

6. Accomplishments & Results, *not* Duties & Responsibilities
7. Highlighting Skills that Support the Announcement
8. Including Recognitions
9. Demonstrating Knowledge of Policies, Procedures and Customer Services Policies

Section 3 - How and Why?

RESUME FOCUSING TECHNIQUES
Skills and Talents for the Future Federal Workforce

10. Skills and Talents for the Future Federal Workforce
11. Do You Share the Agency's Mission and Culture?
12. Targeting with a Profile (Skills) Statement

Section 4 – Putting it All Together

Your Transition into the Future Federal Workforce

JOB INFORMATION

❏ Announcement number, and title and grade(s) of the job for which you are applying

PERSONAL INFORMATION

❏ Full name, mailing address *(with ZIP Code)* and day and evening phone numbers *(with area code)*
❏ Social Security Number
❏ Country of citizenship *(Most Federal jobs require United States citizenship.)*
❏ Veterans' preference *(See reverse.)*
❏ Reinstatement eligibility *(If requested, attach SF 50 proof of your career or career-conditional status.)*
❏ Highest Federal civilian grade held *(Also give job series and dates held.)*

Exercise 1.

Job Information & Personal Data

Formatting job and personal information is an important first step in writing your Federal Resume.

- Make your name stand out in large or bold print
- Make your contact information scannable
- Ensure that federal compliance information is quickly accessible

---

ROBERTA A. SPENCER

Address:	124 3rd Street, NE
	Washington, DC 20002
Telephones:	Home: (202) 566-8910
	Work: (202) 267-9976
	e-mail: spencer@ari.net
Social Security Number:	345-57-6540
Citizenship:	U.S.
Federal Civilian Status:	Public Affairs Specialist, GS-12
Veteran's Status:	N/A
Objective:	International Aviation Officer, GS-0301-13/14
	Announcement No: AWA-AIA-96-1379-10590

Roberta A. Spencer

124 3rd Street, NE
Washington, DC 20002

Home: (202) 5676-8910   Work: (202) 267-9976
e-mail: spencer@ari.net

Social Security Number:	345-57-6540
Citizenship:	U.S.
Federal Civilian Status:	Public Affairs Specialist, GS-12
Veteran's Status:	N/A
Objective:	International Aviation Officer, GS-0301-13/14
	Announcement No: AWA-AIA-96-1379-10590

For additional Personal and Job Information samples, see
The Federal Resume Guidebook
Pages 12-13; sample resumes in Appendix

Personal Data

Full name: _____

Mailing address: *street, city, state & zip* _____

Day telephone: _____   Evening telephone: _____

e-mail: _____

Social Security number: _____

Country of citizenship: _____

Veteran's preference: _____

Reinstatement eligibility: _____

Highest Federal civilian grade held: _____   Dates: _____

Job Information

Objective: *Title of position and Vacancy Announcement Number*

_____

_____

Exercise 2.

Education

EDUCATION

❑ High school
   Name, city, and State *(ZIP Code if known)*
   Date of diploma or GED
❑ Colleges and universities
   Name, city, and State *(ZIP Code if known)*
   Majors
   Type and year of any degrees received
   (If no degree, show total credits earned and indicate whether semester or quarter hours.)
❑ Send a copy of your college transcript only if the job vacancy announcement requests it.

- Placement of the education section on the resume is optional: at the beginning - particularly if your degree is recent or job-related - or following the employment section.

- Suggested format for continuing degree studies:

University of California, Los Angeles, CA 95701
Completed 64 credit hours toward B.S. degree in Speech and Communications, 1989 to present

Or, if you've been working on a degree over the years through several institutions:

Completed 64 credit hours toward B.S. degree in Speech/Communications, 1989-present
University of Maryland, College Park; Anne Arundel Community College, Annapolis, MD; and University of Baltimore, Baltimore, MD

EDUCATION:

Pepperdine University, Los Angeles, CA 97801
Completed 32 hours in post-graduate studies, Education, 1991 - present

San Francisco State University, San Francisco, CA 96810
Master of Arts, Political Science, June 1973

University of California, Los Angeles, CA 95701
Bachelor of Arts, Speech and Communications, June 1971

Simi Valley Community College, Los Angeles, CA 95701
Associate of Arts, June 1969

Robert Fulton High School, Queens, NY 10065
Diploma, 1967

- Include significant academic honors, activities, scholarships, awards, internships, residencies, major papers, thesis, course concentration; list following your degree and date of graduation.

Education

For additional Education samples, see
The Federal Resume Guidebook
Pages 15-20; sample resumes in Appendix

Graduate or Professional School

Name: _____

City, state, zip code: _____

Degree earned: _____ Date: _____

Major: _____

Key subjects/courses/specialties: _____

_____

_____

Honors/Activities: _____

_____

_____

College

Name: _____

City, state, zip code: _____

Degree earned: _____ Date: _____

Major: _____

Key subjects/courses/specialties: _____

_____

_____

Honors/activities: _____

_____

_____

Technical/Vocational/Trade School

Name: _____

City, state, zip code: _____

Credential earned: _____ Date: _____

Honors: _____

High School

Name: _____

City, state, zip code: _____

Diploma/GED: _____ Date: _____

Honors: _____

Exercise 3.

Training

OTHER QUALIFICATIONS

❑ **Job-related** training courses *(title and year)*
❑ **Job-related** skills, for example, other languages, computer software/hardware, tools, machinery, typing speed
❑ **Job-related** certificates and licenses *(current only)*
❑ **Job-related** honors, awards, and special accomplishments, for example, publica– tions, memberships in professional or honor societies, leadership activities, public speaking, and performance awards *(Give dates but do not send documents unless requested.)*

- Your training list (Professional Development) can be organized into major skill areas targeting your announcement and career interests.

- Major areas include: computers, budgets, leadership, EEO, supervision, accounting, management.

- Include title of course and year. Classroom hours are optional, but recommended if over 16.

PROFESSIONAL DEVELOPMENT:

Aviation Technical Courses:	**Hours**
Detail, FAA Civil Aviation Security Office (1995)	3 months, full-time
Air Traffic Control History (1994)	16 hours
Managing Public Communication, FAA Center for Management Development (1993)	8 hours
Introduction to Emergency Readiness (1995)	24 hours

Management Development Courses: (All 1994)

Seven Habits of Highly Effective People	7 days
Discovering Diversity and Valuing the Diverse Workforce	3 hours
The Quality Advantage	8 hours
Management Skills for Non-Supervisors	8 hours
Investment in Excellence	16 hours
Thinking Beyond the Boundaries	4 hours

Communications Training:

Public Involvement Training (1991)	16 hours
Collateral Duty Recruiter Training (1990)	24 hours
Constructive Communications (1988)	8 hours
Communications Training Workshop (1989)	8 hours

Training

For additional Training samples, see
The Federal Resume Guidebook
Pages 20, 146, 151, 153, 156, 159-160, 163

Write your functional areas of professional training and/or major training programs here. Begin with the most recent, and work backwards.

Identify key categories, for example:

Leadership
Supervision
Management
Budget
Accounting
Acquisition and Contracting
Law Enforcement
Computer Skills

_____

_____

_____

_____

_____

_____

_____

_____

_____

_____

_____

_____

_____

_____

_____

Exercise 4.

Other Qualifications

OTHER QUALIFICATIONS

❏ **Job-related** training courses *(title and year)*

❏ **Job-related** skills, for example, other languages, computer software/hardware, tools, machinery, typing speed

❏ **Job-related** certificates and licenses *(current only)*

❏ **Job-related** honors, awards, and special accomplishments, for example, publica–tions, memberships in professional or honor societies, leadership activities, public speaking, and performance awards *(Give dates but do not send documents unless requested.)*

- This section is similar to Item 29 on the SF-171, Other Qualifications and Skills.

- Information here is important for consideration of your additional skills and qualifications, and to review other activities, organizations and interests in your life.

- Emphasize job-related qualifications and memberships.

PROFESSIONAL PUBLICATIONS:

Co-author, *Women & Minorities in Aviation in Hawaii*, Hawaii Office of Education, 1994
Aviation Progress in the Pacific, *FAA World*, October, 1995

PROFESSIONAL PRESENTATIONS:

Hawaii Conference on Women and Minorities
National Congress on Aviation & Space Education

PROFESSIONAL MEMBERSHIPS & AFFILIATIONS:

Air Traffic Advisory Committee (Chair: 1994-95)
Air Force Association
Hawaii Aerospace Development Corporation
Federal Women's Program

HONORS & AWARDS:

Outstanding Performance Ratings seven consecutive years, 1989-1995
National Award for Excellence in Aerospace Education from Civil Air Patrol, 1995

Other Qualifications

For additional Other Qualifications samples, see
The Federal Resume Guidebook
Pages 21-29, 140, 142, 145, 150, 151, 154, 157, 160, 167

List Your Resume Headings for the Other Qualifications Section:

Associations
Community Service
Computer Skills
Conferences Attended
Consultancies

Honors & Awards
International Travel
Languages
Memberships/Offices
Part-time Teaching Positions

Presentations
Publications
Special Interests/Activities
Volunteer Services

_____

_____

_____

_____

_____

_____

_____

_____

_____

_____

_____

_____

_____

_____

_____

_____

_____

_____

_____

_____

_____

_____

Exercise 5.

Work Experience

WORK EXPERIENCE

❑ Give the following information for your paid and nonpaid work experience related to the job for which you are applying. *(Do not send job descriptions.)*

    Job title *(include series and grade if Federal job)*

    Duties and accomplishments

    Employer's name and address

    Supervisor's name and phone number

    Starting and ending dates *(month and year)*

    Hours per week

    Salary

❑ Indicate if we may contact your current supervisor.

Preparing an Outline of Positions

- **Include federal compliance details for the past ten years.** Begin with your most recent position and work backwards.

- For positions held more than ten years ago, edit and select most important duties/achievements.

- Prior to ten years, supervisor's name, telephone number, specific address, zip codes and salaries may not be relevant, correct or needed any longer. Provide information only if it is accurate.

Format Suggestion for Saving Space:

- If you have worked for a single agency at the same location for an extended time, use a simplified block to display the agency information at the start of a series of positions:

FEDERAL AVIATION ADMINISTRATION   **May 1983 to present**
800 Independence Avenue, SW, Washington, DC 20591

    Deputy Public Affairs Officer, GS-1082-12/4   (October 1993 to Present)
    Supervisor: Mr. Roger Sperrin (202) 267-9975   Current Salary: $47,165
    Supervisor may be contacted.   Starting Salary: $35,136
    Insert description of responsibilities and accomplishments.

    Public Affairs Specialist, GS-1035-11/12   (October 1991 – 1993)
    FAA Aviation Education Program Manager   Starting Salary: $29,876
    Supervisor: William Leytle (202) 267-8338   Ending Salary: $31,352

DEPARTMENT OF DEFENSE   **1985 - 1991**
Pacific Air Command

    Assistant Command Historian, GS-9   (October 1988 – 1991)
    The Pentagon, Washington, DC 20330   Starting Salary: $24,865
    Supervisor: LTG Robt. Pakenser (Ret.) no known phone   Ending Salary: $27,546

    Research Historian   (September 1985 – 1988)
    Hawaii Naval Air Station, Honolulu, HI   Starting Salary: $21,156
    Supervisor: John Clayton (808) 546-7785   Ending Salary: $23,652

Work Experience

For additional Work Experience samples, see
The Federal Resume Guidebook
Page 30, sample resumes in Appendix

Develop an outline of positions held in this space in order to plan the number of job-related positions held within the last 10 years; and positions held previously which will be included without compliance details and limited description.

Employer 1.

Office

Address _____ Zip _____

Supervisor's name _____ Tel. ( ) _____

Supervisor may (may not) be contacted.

Title of position _____ GS Series _____ Grade _____

Beginning Salary _____ Current Salary _____ Hrs./wk. _____

Employer 2.

Office

Address _____ Zip _____

Supervisor's name _____ Tel. ( ) _____

Title of position _____ GS Series _____ Grade _____

Beginning Salary _____ Ending Salary _____ Hrs./wk. _____

Employer 3.

Office

Address _____ Zip _____

Supervisor's name _____ Tel. ( ) _____

Title of position _____ GS Series _____ Grade _____

Beginning Salary _____ Ending Salary _____ Hrs./wk. _____

Continue on a separate sheet, if needed.

Today's Resume Focus Must Be On:

ACCOMPLISHMENTS AND RESULTS –

not merely a description of the duties and responsibilities that you performed. Include details of your projects or programs.

PROGRAMS AND POLICIES THAT SERVE -

specific people (customers), not just a generalized public, or functions of job responsibilities.

DEVELOPING SKILLS -

that will be required in the next century, not limited to serving today's needs. Emphasize skills that you will need in your next position, not simply a list of your present skills.

DESCRIBING ACCOMPLISHMENTS -

in dynamic terms demonstrating that you have made a difference in your organization, not merely writing about activities.

Writing Your Job Descriptions

Introduction

The following series of exercises is intended to assist you in acquiring the skills and the focus necessary to describe your responsibilities in ways that will increase the attention they receive from potential managers.

The changes affecting all workplaces have reached the federal sector and it is vital to develop the ability to communicate in terms demanded by today's employment conditions.

Section 2 – WRITING YOUR JOB DESCRIPTIONS
Selling Yourself!

6.   Accomplishments & Results, *not* Duties & Responsibilities
7.   Highlighting Skills that Support the Announcement
8.   Including Recognitions
9.   Demonstrating Knowledge of Policies, Procedures and Customer Service Policies

Section 3 - RESUME FOCUSING TECHNIQUES

10. Skills and Talents for the Future Federal Workforce
11. Do You Share the Agency's Mission and Culture?
12. Targeting with a Profile Statement

Section 4 - PUTTING IT ALL TOGETHER
Your Transition into the Future Federal Workforce

Exercise 6.

<u>*Accomplishments & Results*, not *Duties & Responsibilities*</u>

- Your resume invariably builds upon what you have done, but effective resumes don't merely present functions -- ***THEY COMMUNICATE RESULTS!***

- The **Government Performance and Results Act of 1993** will, by 1997, force agencies to develop performance measures for their key mission results.

- Effective vacancy announcements will increasingly convey job expectations in terms of the results that agencies expect to achieve.

- And, effective federal resumes will have to convey the applicant's ability to achieve those results if they are going to lead to the federal jobs of the future.

- *Examples of results-oriented statements include:*

  - Presentations resulted in major international coverage for innovative technologies in air commerce.
  - Media briefings secured positive editorials for major safety regulation initiative, resulting in favorable coverage in national print and broadcast media.
  - Achieved substantial public awareness of impact of new trade agreements on international transportation systems.

EXAMPLE OF JOB DESCRIPTION, WITH AN EMPHASIS ON DETAILS/RESULTS:

Organized 50th anniversary reunion of more than 100 veterans from the 11th Air Force who fought in Hawaii during World War II. The event included three days of activities on Pearl Harbor Naval Station and highlighted a 45-minute video featuring many of the attendees in vintage film footage. Arranged lodging, meals, and transportation, and conducted exit interviews with 80 percent of participants before departure. Convention cited by Air Force Association Historical Society.

Designed and managed construction of two foyer exhibits for Command Headquarters. Identified key command achievements over a fifty-year period, researched print and photo archives to ensure accuracy and attractiveness of presentation. Exhibits averaged 50 square-feet and included historical information on the military in Hawaii in a compatible environment with local wildlife displays.

Published more than four significant historical articles per year based on research. Coordinated meetings of local historical association and negotiated command support for multi-media presentations.

Accomplishments & Results

For additional Projects and Results samples, see
The Federal Resume Guidebook
Pages 30-58, 104-108 (SES core factors);
149, 152, 155, 157-158, 165-166, 169-170, 172-185 (KSAs).

Developing a Project List

When writing your position descriptions, instead of trying to remember all of your responsibilities, concentrate on the major projects or programs to which you contributed. Describe the role you played in the project (leader, co-leader, member of team).

1. Project/Program

Title of Project/Program:

Budget (if relevant):

Role you played:

Mission, objective, purpose of project:

Customer/vendor:

Who you communicated or worked with to complete project:

Major challenge(s) or problem(s) during project:

Results (i.e., cost savings, increased efficiency, improved service to customers)

2. Project/Program

Title of Project/Program:

Budget (if relevant):

Role you played:

Mission, objective, purpose of project:

Customer/vendor:

Who you communicated or worked with to complete project:

Major challenge(s) or problem(s) during project:

Results (i.e., cost savings, increased efficiency, improved service to customers)

REVIEW:
1   Be sure to highlight your contribution to a notable result.
2.   Emphasize ways in which you demonstrated skills required in the advertised job.
3.   Review the job announcement. Can you provide two accomplishments for each critical job element?

Exercise 7.

Highlighting Skills that Support the Announcement

- The most important element of any position description is to make certain that the skills that you choose to highlight make sense in terms of the position for which you are applying. This is where the analysis of the vacancy announcement is most important.

- If the resume is a good fit for the position that you are seeking, it will reinforce your qualifications at every opportunity.

- The best way to achieve this is to demonstrate that your previous activities include accomplishments that relate to the potential employer's needs.

EXAMPLE 1.

Sentence from Position Description: Responsible for program planning including requirements definition, acquiring, implementation of the Navy-wide Computer Aided Engineering and Documentation System contract.

Resume statement including specific skills/achievements demonstrating skills that support the announcement: Awarded the CAEDOS contract for $62.7M in less than 11 months, without a protest. Brought state-of-the-art CAD/CAM equipment to the Navy at a 50-60% in savings. The contract was the largest single CAD/CAM contract ever, when it was awarded.

EXAMPLE 2.

Sentence from Job Announcement: Conduct procurement planning and negotiation.

Resume statement using job announcement language demonstrating skills that support the announcement: Conduct procurement plans and negotiate terms and conditions for twelve innovative Blanket Purchase Agreements (BPAs) which provide Navy and other DoD customers the latest commercial technology at discount prices, with minimum administrative cost and effort.

- **Check on skills that you have developed which support a proposed announcement:**

  - Review the critical skills listed on your vacancy announcement.

  - Identify the ways in which you have demonstrated those skills in your most recent positions, or where recent training has prepared you for additional responsibilities in related areas.

  - **Remember, in seeking promotion or career changes, your critical challenge is to demonstrate that success at previous positions is preparation for success at the next position.**

Highlighting Skills

For additional skill set samples, see
The Federal Resume Guidebook
Pages 21-24, 28-29, 51, 54, 58, 92, 95, 104-108
Resumes in Appendix, see pages: 140, 142, 143, 148, 151, 152,
154, 157, 160, 165, 167, 168

Take a line from your current position description or a job announcement. Rewrite in terms of results, rather than function. Focus on skills/achievements related to target jobs.

Sentence from position description:

_____

_____

_____

_____

Rewrite with specific details:

_____

_____

_____

_____

Sentence from job announcement:

_____

_____

_____

_____

Sentence for resume including job announcement terminology:

_____

_____

_____

_____

REVIEW:

The critical concern to personnel specialists is progressively responsible experience. More recent jobs should reflect actions involving more complex assignments, at higher levels in the organization.

1. Do your summaries highlight your most recent experiences?
2. Do they convince a selecting official that you are the right person for this position?

Exercise 8.

Including Recognitions in Job Descriptions

- The federal resume instructions contained in the OF-510 say, "Do not include Letters of Commendation or Award documents unless requested."

- The descriptions of your positions in the resume should not rely solely on what you did. If you have earned ***outstanding performance ratings, agency awards, employee of the month citations, or any other form of distinction,*** this is the section to link the awards that you have received with the functions that you did.

- No section of the resume should stand in isolation, and federal resumes are especially strengthened when the awards that you have earned over the years are linked to the work that you did to earn them. Do not think solely in terms of agency awards!

- Honors from outside organizations, recognition for community service, achievements from your academic or civic background can also reinforce recognition of your skills.

- Similarly, publications or presentations can provide corroborating evidence of these abilities.

EXAMPLES OF LANGUAGE WHICH INCLUDE RECOGNITIONS AND AWARDS IN THE JOB DESCRIPTION SECTION OF YOUR FEDERAL RESUME.

- Received Letter of Commendation from the Chief of Naval Material, 1982.

- Planning, acquiring and implementing a CAD/CAM system at 54 Navy sites. Received a "Special Act Award" for all my accomplishments under this project.

- National Performance Review (NPR) Hammer Award for Acquisition Reform, 1996 Participation in the DoD EC/EDI Process Action Team.

- Received overall performance rating of "outstanding" for accomplishments during this project. Also, received a letter of appreciation from NAWCWPNS, China Lake, CA, for my accomplishments in handling of "Past Performance".

- Organized 50th anniversary reunion of over 100 veterans from the 11th Air Force who fought in Hawaii during World War II. Convention cited by Air Force Association Historical Society.

- Developed and implemented budgetary requirements and procedures for media campaigns. Scheduled annual calendar for the Public Affairs Office. Devised and implemented components and timelines for strengthened general aviation safety component in FAA's Aviation Education program. Campaign cited by AOPA for reducing general aviation accident rate during 1993.

Including Recognitions

For additional samples of Recognitions cited in resume text, see
The Federal Resume Guidebook
Pages 28-29, 47, 58

List your Awards / Recognitions and the activities that have earned it.
List most recent awards first.

1. _____

_____

_____

_____

_____

2. _____

_____

_____

_____

_____

3. _____

_____

_____

_____

_____

4. _____

_____

_____

_____

_____

5. _____

_____

_____

_____

_____

REVIEW:
1. Is the list complete?
2. Can you link the awards to specific activities, responsibilities, or projects?
3. Can you link these awards to the critical job elements on the vacancy announcement?

Exercise 9.

Demonstrating Knowledge of Programs, Procedures and Customer Services Policies

- This is the element that can be most important in conveying to evaluators your knowledge of the **procedures** to get the job done.

- If you are seeking to change career paths, it is especially important to demonstrate an understanding of the **procedures** that will be required in the new field.

- Moving from line responsibilities to management, or from managing one function to another, usually requires convincing potential supervisors that you have the capabilities that will be important at the next level.

- As always, the most important factor in any presentation must be in terms of the new position's requirements.

- With reinvention programs, it is important to acknowledge who your customers are, your interest in serving them better, and your role in improving service and efficiency.

THREE EXAMPLES OF STATEMENTS INCORPORATING KNOWLEDGE OF POLICIES AND PROCEDURES WITH AWARENESS OF CUSTOMER SERVICE:

Contract Specialist with the multi-service Standard Procurement Systems (SPS) acquisition. The scope of the SPS contract is to obtain commercially available software, training and services deployed to approximately 1,000 procurement activities located throughout the world.

Direct the day-to-day operations of the Command's enterprise network to ensure operational readiness and timely support to the functional users.

Work with project managers/technical staff with customer entities to accomplish advance acquisition planning; conduct reviews and analyses of procurement requests, technical requirements and statements of work.

Demonstrating Knowledge of Programs, Procedures and Customer Service Policies

For additional resume text samples describing programs,
procedures & customer services policies, see
The Federal Resume Guidebook, pages 38-45, 51, 58
Recommended reading: *The Blair House Papers,* NPR

For each of the critical functions that you perform (or have identified on your vacancy announcement), identify your role in performing the function.

Focus on the persons, organizations, or groups of citizens who most directly receive the products of your activities. Describe what you have delivered to them, and the difference that your work has made to them.

1. **Who are your customers?**

_____

_____

_____

_____

2. **What are your major programs?**

_____

_____

_____

_____

_____

3. **What procedures do you follow or have expert knowledge of?**

_____

_____

_____

_____

_____

REVIEW:
1. Do these skills support the job announcement?
2. Are these the skills/achievements that led to awards?

Exercise 10.

Skills and Talents for the Future Federal Workforce

- Your critical concern is to identify the skills and talents that you have that will position you for the federal workforce of the future.

- The skills that secured federal positions ten years ago will not do for the federal workforce of the twenty-first century.

- Your perspective as you plan to write a resume must be to look back at your career and identify the things about you that have changed as you begin the steps toward defining your position in that twenty-first century workforce.

SAMPLE RESUME TEXT:

Before: Due to a shortage of personnel, I conducted a month-long detail in FAA's Office of Public Affairs in Los Angeles, CA, during which I assumed all responsibilities of the Public Affairs Officer in the second largest media market in the United States.

After: Managed month-long detail in FAA's Los Angeles Public Affairs Office to provide major market coverage of sensitive issues involving U.S. agencies and Asian-Pacific nations. Achieved substantial public awareness of impact of new trade agreements on international transportation systems.

Remember . . .

The potential employer is much less interested in what you have done . . . than in what you can do to <u>fill the need</u> within another organization (or to demonstrate your abilities for the next promotion).

Skills and Talents for the Future Federal Workforce

Write three critical skills you can bring to your next employer that will contribute to the success of their organization's mission. Be sure to describe them in terms of the results that others experienced as a result of your action. Use measures that support your claims.

Examples:

- <u>Achieved substantial public awareness</u> of impact of new trade agreements on international transportation systems.

- <u>Established systematic procedures</u> to solicit reader input and produce a cost-effective product that kept employees knowledgeable about agency issues and programs. Innovations in on-line production technology cut distribution time by one-third while realizing 20 percent cost savings.

Critical Skill (i.e. Verbal communications, negotiations) _____

_____

_____

_____

_____

Critical Skill (i.e. Initiation, coordination and monitoring programs) _____

_____

_____

_____

_____

Critical Skill (i.e. Supervision) _____

_____

_____

_____

_____

REVIEW:
1. Do these skills support your application?
2. Repeat process for all positions in past ten years.

Exercise 11.

Do You Share the Agency's Mission and Culture?

- Personnel Specialists may evaluate applications for positions of public trust and responsibility to assess whether the applicant shares the agency's mission and culture.

- People applying from within the agency will understand, as a result of their experience, the common terminology of the agency.

- The vacancy announcement is the best available guide to the elements of the agency's mission that are important in evaluating the application.

SAMPLE ANNOUNCEMENT DUTIES:

Responsible for planning and developing policies and activities related to the FAA's international program; analyzing data; and conducting studies which support those policies and activities; organizing, executing and managing activities; implementing the FAA's international policies and programs; and supporting the overall activities of the Division and office.

SAMPLE RESUME TEXT:

Before: Fulfill all the responsibilities of the official spokesperson for the FAA Headquarters in the absence of the Public Affairs Officer. Provide the public, using the news media as the principal intermediary, with information about the agency's mission, policies, and operations.

After: (1) Represent FAA Headquarters before general media in the absence of the Public Affairs Officer. Coordinated seven-person branch providing public information about the agency's mission, policies, and operations to ensure timely and responsive presentation of sensitive issues of aviation policy and technology. Earned recognition from both print and electronic media for professionalism of briefings and quick responses to technical topics.

(2) Promoted and encouraged partnerships with businesses, education, and government organizations involving aviation activities. Enhanced development of a multi-agency commitment to the aviation education program that reached several thousand students each year. New pilot licensing in Headquarters region increased 7 percent annually during this program.

Agency Mission

Define your understanding of your agency's mission:

_____
_____
_____
_____
_____

Agency Culture

Define your understanding of what traits the agency values in employees:

_____
_____
_____
_____
_____

Describe three of your achievements/skills that demonstrate your understanding of the agency's mission and your commitment to its culture.

1. _____
_____
_____
_____

2. _____
_____
_____
_____

3. _____
_____
_____
_____

REVIEW:
1   Do these traits fit well in your application strategy?
2. Do these achievements reflect skills critical to future duties?

Exercise 12.

Writing a Profile Statement

- The federal resume format allows you to strengthen your application by summarizing your qualifications in an opening statement, an option that the blocks and data of the old SF-171 never permitted.

- This section can be labeled "Profile," or "Professional Profile," or "Background Summary," or "Qualifications Summary," or any other description that suits you.

- The critical factor in this section is to introduce yourself to the reader in terms of the qualifications stressed in the vacancy announcement.

- Very often, in job interviews, an employer will open by saying, "Tell me about yourself."

- This block on the federal resume provides an opportunity to develop a precise and targeted response.

SAMPLE RESUME TEXT:

Format 1:
PROFILE:
Aviation communications professional with over 15 years experience demonstrating organizational skills, award-winning media relations, and development and maintenance of positive relationships among government employees, industry representatives, and academia. Recent assignments include special project involving Pacific region air transportation technology and multiple agency missions. Adept at reviewing, analyzing, and maintaining government and private industry programs, budgets, and collateral materials with international effects.

Format 2 *(Listing of critical skills as the introductory "profile" statement)*
SUMMARY OF QUALIFICATIONS:
- Over 15 years experience as Aviation Communications Professional.
- Exceptional organizational and project management skills, including multiple agency missions and regional projects.
- Award-winning media relations experience includes print and broadcast coverage
- Effective in developing and maintaining positive relationships among government employees, industry representatives, and academia.
- Adept at reviewing, analyzing, and maintaining government and private industry programs, budgets, and collateral materials with international effects.

Profile Statement

For additional resume samples with profile statement, see
The Federal Resume Guidebook
Pages 5-7, 21-22, Sample Resumes, pages 143-168

To write a Summary of Skills, create a list of your significant skills targeting the announcement. To write the Profile for your resume, answer the following three questions.

1. What is the single or major characteristic(s) that I most want the employer to know about me?

_____
_____
_____
_____

2. What features of my background are most likely to distinguish me from other applicants? (This is an _important_ question – think about this!)

_____
_____
_____
_____

3. What is the most important factor(s) within my qualifications that matches the skills sought for this position?

_____
_____
_____
_____

Combine these responses into an answer to the statement: "Tell me about yourself."

_____
_____
_____
_____
_____
_____

REVIEW:
1. Does this summary reflect skills and perspective in the job announcement?
2. Does this summary highlight my most important qualifications?

Putting It All Together

Organizing a resume can be one of the most challenging tasks that an applicant performs, and it can make all the difference between a successful presentation and an application that merely ranks among the many qualified applicants.

When organizing your resume, *prioritize the information.* Review the position announcement, and think in terms of two factors:

- **First, what are my strongest skills?**
- **Second, what skills does the announcement emphasize?**

A federal resume is an advertisement of your candidacy for a particular position. Ideally, your qualifications will fit identically with the skills desired by the employer. *To make certain that the employer recognizes the fit, it can help to present the essential information up front, and save less vital details for later.*

Most people learned to write a resume in a college placement office when they were approaching graduation. Then, people were taught to list education first, because it is the leading qualification of a person who has little other experience. Fifteen years later, the education section should no longer be the strongest qualification on your resume. Your resume should convince potential employers that what you have done lately is very important for them.

Many sections of the resume are optional.

- A **profile** can prepare the reader to look for the information that you want to emphasize.

- A **summary of key accomplishments** can be used to stress your successes that are relevant to the position.

- Some information about ability to use **computers** (at least word processing and spreadsheets) can convey an impression of recent skills that are considered important for managers.

- Ability to read, write, and speak **foreign languages** can be invaluable in some positions -- such as the one advertised -- and these skills should be mentioned if they are credible.

If any of these sections, however, lead you to wonder whether you are stretching the limits of credibility, they are better off omitted than sinking an application. A "Professional Training" section, for example, that demonstrates that you have spent more than three months each year in classes of one kind or another might cause some managers to wonder whether you will spend enough time at your desk.

To the best of your ability, arrange your information so that it sells you best for the position for which you are applying. That could mean, of course, **modifying the organization slightly for each application.** The position, if you get it, will require several years of your professional life. *If it is not worth appropriate restructuring of your resume, it's probably not the job for you anyway.*

The advertisement used as a model for this workbook lists three critical job elements as leading qualifications. In simplified form, they are:

(1) Program management
(2) International aviation technical and operational support
(3) Coordinating sensitive and complex information with internal and external groups.

This is a position announcement that emphasizes **experience** as the key method of demonstrating all of the job elements that will be used as ranking factors. Therefore, **job experience should be the leading portion of the resume,** and the candidate whose resume we are using as a model has extensive, relevant experience.

A candidate with different qualifications might want to organize the information differently. For example, an airways facilities engineer might want to emphasize technical skills and related program management responsibilities, perhaps by devoting additional detail to professional training courses and/or by moving the "Education and Training" section of the resume ahead of some of the early career experiences that required more technical knowledge and less managerial skill. Alternatively, an applicant with an extensive engineering background might need to spend more effort highlighting the ability to represent the agency before internal and external groups (if only to overcome reviewers' doubts that engineers have sufficient skills in this area).

Three ways of organizing a resume for this vacancy announcement, depending on professional expertise, are:

Optional Organization No. 1:
Public Affairs Specialist
Use of Selected Major Accomplishments to highlight relevant experience and an emphasis on Professional Experience

Optional Organization No. 2:
Airways Facilities Engineer
Emphasis on Technical Skills and Related Program Management Responsibilities by highlighting Education and Training.

Format Option 3:
Senior Engineer
Highlight the ability to represent the agency before internal and external groups.

A "Reinvention" Resume Writing Tip

Do these reinvention programs and concepts work for you?
Can you write about them in your resume?

Improved accountability –
➢ Have you improved accountability?
➢ Can this success be measured by savings?

Administrative simplification –
➢ Have you streamlined processes, eliminated micromanagement, and reduced wasteful paperwork?
➢ Have you participated in the creation of a one-stop shop or served as a single point of contact?

Identify your customers and win them over – Have you:
➢ Increased the time for service to customers?
➢ Improved customer satisfaction?
➢ Cut backlog and response time?
➢ Delivered new services in response to customer need?
➢ Provided more efficient and accurate access to information via electronic records?

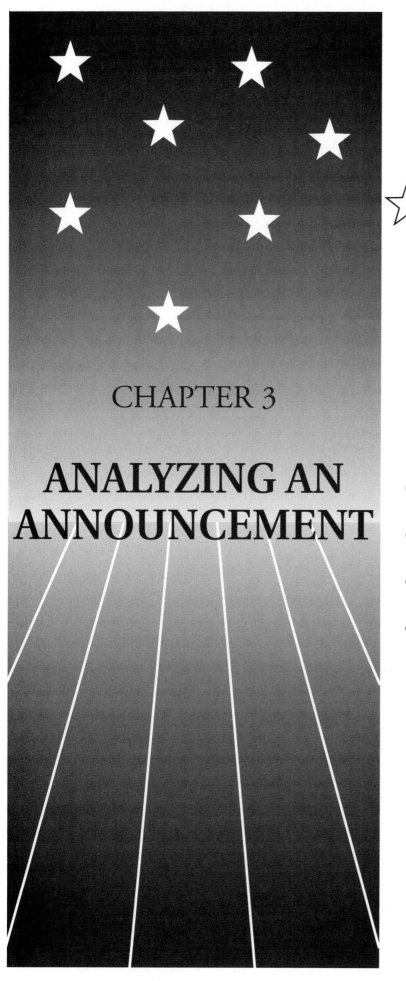

CHAPTER 3

ANALYZING AN ANNOUNCEMENT

- Interpretation

- Announcement

- KSAs

- Evaluation Criteria

Department of Transportation
Federal Aviation Administration
Promotional and Career Opportunities
AWA-AIA-96 -1379-10590

Open Date: Jul 10, 1996
Close Date: Jul 30, 1996
Position: INTERNATIONAL AVIATION OPERATIONS SPECIALIST, GS-0301-13/14
Location: Washington, DC
Organization Location:
　　FAA Washington Headquarters Region, Assistant Administrator for Policy Planning and Int'l Aviation, Office of Int'l Aviation, Asia/Pacific Division, AIA-400
Area of Consideration:
　　Washington Metro Area
Duties:
　　Responsible for planning and developing policies and activities related to the FAA's international program; analyzing and data; conducting studies which support those policies and activities; organizing, executing and managing activities; implementing the FAA's international policies and programs; and supporting the overall activities of the Division and office.

QUALIFICATIONS:
　　All applicants must demonstrate one year of specialized experience equivalent to the next lower grade in the Federal government. Specialized experience is experience which is in or directly related to the line of work of the position to be filled and which has equipped the applicant with the particular knowledge, skills and abilities to successfully perform the duties of the position. To be creditable, specialized experience must have been equivalent to the next lower grade in the normal line of progression for the occupation in the organization.

Evaluation criteria:
　　Eligible candidates will be ranked based on the knowledge, skills, abilities, and other characteristics (KSAO's), described below.

RATING AND RANKING FACTORS: (KSA's)

1. Skill in applying program management concepts.

2. Skill in coordinating international aviation technical/operational support programs.

3. Skill in coordinating sensitive/complex issues with internal/external organizations.

4. Skill in written communication.

5. Skill in oral communication.

Promotion Potential: To the GS-14.

NOTE: Certain handicapped individuals and disabled veterans eligible for special appointing authorities may also apply. Ingrade/downgrade applicants will be considered.

NOTE: THIS ANNOUNCEMENT MAY BE USED TO FILL OTHER SIMILAR POSITIONS SUBJECT TO THE PRIOR APPROVAL OF THE HUMAN RESOURCE MANAGEMENT DIVISION.

NOTE: EQUAL OPPORTUNITY THROUGH AFFIRMATIVE ACTION: The Federal Aviation Administration is committed to a multi-cultural environment. Minorities and women and strongly encouraged to apply.

D. HOW TO APPLY

You may submit a resume, an Application for Federal Employment, SF-171 (6/88 or later edition); Optional Application for Federal Employment, OF-612; or any written application that contains the information reflected on the attachment entitled "Application Format." NOTE: If you choose to submit the SF-171, you are no longer required to complete questions 38-47. Basic qualifications for the position will be determined solely from the information included on the application, which must be complete and up-to-date.

On a separate sheet of bond paper, you may provide additional information regarding your possession of the KSAOs for this position. (Optional - Not required, however, it provides applicants the opportunity to describe portions of their experience, training, education, etc., which are directly related to the KSAO). The information will be used for ranking of applicants after basic eligibility is determined. For each KSAO listed above, provide the following information : 1) Work Experience: Describe the tasks you have performed which demonstrate the KSAO, giving the dates, places, and positions where you did this. 2) Education, Training and/or Awards: Describe training, education, and/or awards you have received which demonstrate the KSA, including the dates you received the training, education, and/or awards. 3) Other Information, such as: Volunteer experience, hobbies, etc., which demonstrate the KSAOs, giving the dates and places where you did this.

Supervisory evaluation of KSA's

Evaluation of Knowledge, Skills and Abilities, completed by supervisor (current or former).
A completed SF-181, Race and National Origin Identification Form.

WHERE TO SEND APPLICATIONS:

Federal Aviation Administration
Human Resource Management Division
Operations Team One, AHR-19A
800 Independence Avenue, S.W.
Washington, D.C. 20591
Applications may be hand-delivered to Room 109.

All applications must be received by the closing date of this announcement.
Please call (202) 267-8007 for additional information.

Excepted Service:

On April 1, 1996 the Federal Aviation Administration (FAA) created a new personnel system, the Federal Aviation Service (FAS). The FAS excepts the FAA from most traditional Federal personnel laws. Basic Federal employee benefits like retirement, health and life insurance, workers' compensation, and holidays will remain the same for FAA employees as for other Federal employees. Present Federal employees currently occupying positions in the Competitive Service will, if selected for FAA positions, be converted to the Excepted Service under the FAS. Current leave balances and other benefits will be transferred to the FAA.

Privacy Act Requirements (P.L. 93-579): The referenced forms are used to determine qualifications for promotional and career opportunities, and are authorized under Title 5 of U.S. Code, Sections 3302 and 3361.

Each specified form must be submitted in order for you to be considered for promotion to the position being advertised. The social security number is not required for this purpose and may be deleted from the forms submitted. The servicing human resource management office of the office named in this announcement will be able to provide information on Specific Privacy Act requirements.

DOT is an equal opportunity employer. Selections shall be made regardless of race, color, religion, national origin, sex, age, physical and/or mental handicap, marital or parental status, political or employee organizational affiliation. Applicants who fail to submit required forms will not be considered. Forms requiring signature and date may be reproduced, but must be submitted with original signatures and dates to be accepted. Send only those forms required. None of these forms will be subsequently loaned or returned to the applicant.

Use of postage-paid Government envelopes to file job applications is a violation of Federal laws and regulations. Applications submitted in postage-paid Government envelopes will not be considered.

FAA vacancy information and certain application forms are now available on the FAA's World Wide Web site at: http://jobs.faa.gov or by calling our Faxback system at (405) 954-0250.

Announcement Analysis

This chapter provides an analysis of the previous vacancy announcement. Few people will be applying for only one position, and revising your federal resume to address each potential vacancy is much more effort than most people want to devote to a job search. However, if you are applying for several apparently related positions, it will be useful to review your federal resume in terms of the requirements that agencies establish for the types of positions for which you are applying.

The announcement that we selected for this analysis is a real vacancy that was posted by the Federal Aviation Administration during the summer of 1996. We will follow this analysis by reviewing -- and modifying -- the resume of a federal employee who might be interested in the position and considering changes that can be made to strengthen the qualifications. The resume is a conglomerate -- one that was compiled from a few samples and with a few changes critical to place the applicant in the area of consideration for the position.

```
Heading:
            Department of Transportation
          Federal Aviation Administration
        Promotional and Career Opportunities
              AWA-AIA-96 -1379-10590
```

The heading of the announcement presents critical details about the position(s) included in the presentation. It identifies the department (Transportation), component (Federal Aviation Administration) and announcement number. This announcement number should appear on your application, either as a prominent part of the cover letter or as an "Objective" element of your federal resume. If you maintain your federal resume on a computer, revising it to change the objective for each vacancy is a relatively simple procedure. If you want to maintain a consistent resume, conveying the objective or announcement number in the cover letter will in no way jeopardize your application -- unless the vacancy announcement specifically requires that the announcement number be on the application itself.

```
Opening and Closing Dates:
   Open Date:  Jul 10, 1996
   Close Date: Jul 30, 1996
```

These elements are usually straightforward. The opening date shows the date that the agency authorized filling the vacancy, and the closing date indicates the earliest date after which applications may be rejected. All applications received in the appropriate office (usually identified in the "How To Apply" section, below) must be considered. Agencies may extend the closing date, and they often do. Usually, the period between posting an announcement (opening) and closing will be at least two weeks. Many people will not see the posting during that period, and some bulletin boards and other posting sites (websites, for example) are not necessarily cleared on the last day of the posting. When agencies advertise positions for external consideration, and do not get the announcements into suitable professional publications until after an original closing deadline has expired, they will provide opportunities for applicants to submit their documents. If you don't see an application until late in the period (for example, until the day after applications must be submitted), feel free to call this additional information number. If the agency intends to extend the closing date in the announcement, you can take advantage of the additional time.

> **Position:** INTERNATIONAL AVIATION OPERATIONS SPECIALIST, GS-0301-13/14

This item identifies the position title and classification series, in this case: International Aviation Operations Specialist, GS-0301-13/14. The GS-0301 series is a very broad managerial category, and can incorporate a substantial range of qualifications. Although the position is with the Federal Aviation Administration, it does not necessarily require experience as an air traffic controller, an airway systems engineer, or a multitude of other technical skills that can be helpful for advancement in the agency. The 13/14 level, however, indicates that this position is above the normal career-entry level, and will require several years of professional experience.

Each position description will include a job series classification and grade. If you are not certain about the match between your experience and the background usually associated with this series, the agency advertising can provide information about qualifications, the customary grade of others in the position, and any promotion potential or career ladder that is associated with the position. Some announcements will emphasize: "No promotion potential." This notice does not necessarily mean that the position is a career-ender, but once in such a position, the successful applicant will have to search carefully for the next opportunity.

> **Location:** Washington, DC

This item defines the position as Washington, DC based.

> **Organization Location:**
> FAA Washington Headquarters Region, Assistant Administrator for Policy Planning and Int'l Aviation, Office of Int'l Aviation, Asia/Pacific Division, AIA-400

This item specifies that within the FAA's Washington headquarters, the position will be within the Asia/Pacific Division of the Office of International Aviation, which is under the supervision of the Assistant Administration for Policy Planning and International Aviation. More than a physical location, this provides information about the supervisory relationships of the position that can be important in identifying potential supervisors, selecting officials, or the prominence of the organization within the agency's hierarchy. This position is not at the top of the chart, but a successful applicant should be familiar with these dimensions of the organization and the specialized skills (Asia/Pacific) that will be important to highlight in responding to the announcement.

```
Area of Consideration:
  Washington Metro Area
```

This item confirms that the agency will only consider applicants from the Washington metropolitan area. Under the structure of the federal government's Washington metropolitan area, that can include anyone willing to commute to the office on a daily basis. Applicants from as far away as suburban Richmond, Virginia, West Virginia, Baltimore, Maryland, or Delaware can be considered. The limited area of consideration confirms that the agency will not pay relocation expenses for a successful applicant.

This item can range far more broadly than the single area of consideration listed on this announcement. For senior positions, or those where the agency is recruiting candidates and advertising broadly, this area might be listed as "open," or "all sources." In some cases, announcements will indicate "status candidates only," or be limited to candidates from within the Department or agency. If a restricted area of consideration is defined on the announcement, make certain that you indicate clearly that you fall within the area of consideration in submitting your application.

```
Duties:
  Responsible for planning and developing policies and
  activities related to the FAA's international program;
  analyzing and data, and conducting studies which support those
  policies and activities; organizing, executing and managing
  activities; implementing the FAA's international policies and
  programs; and supporting the overall activities of the
  Division and office.
```

This item identifies the primary responsibilities associated with the position. It enumerates the key functions, and any successful federal resume application will have to demonstrate in credible and consistent ways that the applicant has the experience and skills necessary to perform the position. In this instance, the terms "the FAA's international program," and "the FAA's international policies and programs," send a very strong signal that the applicant will need a specialized background in international relations specifically related to the FAA's programs and policies in the Asia/Pacific region. At the same time, the end phrase, "supporting the overall activities of the Division and office," leaves the position open for the applicant to introduce additional talents that might be advantageous for the agency.

```
Qualifications:
  All applicants must demonstrate one year of specialized
  experience equivalent to the next lower grade in the Federal
  government. Specialized experience is experience which is in
  or directly related to the line of work of the position to be
  filled and which has equipped the applicant with the
  particular knowledge, skills and abilities to successfully
  perform the duties of the position. To be creditable,
  specialized experience must have been equivalent to the next
  lower grade in the normal line of progression for the
  occupation in the organization.
```

This item provides general guidance that the successful applicant must demonstrate specialized experience at the next lower grade level. This indicates that the selecting official will have some flexibility in defining the appropriate candidate. Because the announcement describes the position as "13/14," this could involve a promotion opportunity for a GS-12 who has worked on related issues for at least a year, or mobility options for GS-13s or 14s who might be willing to accept a lateral appointment with some promotion potential. The ending line, "To be creditable, specialized experience must have been equivalent to the next lower grade in the normal line of progression for the occupation in the organization" also provides some room for flexibility. An applicant might consider who recently served in the position, or comparable positions within the organization, and ask about their backgrounds. There is no consistent career path for a GS-0301, such as there is for an air traffic control supervisor or a supervisory investigator. What is most important in these conditions is the set of skills that the selecting official considers most required by the position at the time.

```
Evaluation Criteria:
    Eligible candidates will be ranked based on the knowledge,
    skills, abilities, and other characteristics (KSAOs),
    described below.

RATING AND RANKING FACTORS: (KSAs)
    1. Skill in applying program management concepts.
    2. Skill in coordinating international aviation
       technical/operational support programs.
    3. Skill in coordinating sensitive/complex issues with
       internal/ external organizations.
    4. Skill in written communication.
    5. Skill in oral communication.
Promotion Potential:
    To the GS-14.
```

These items are most important for the presentation of your resume because they indicate the qualifications that personnel specialists screening the applications will emphasize in identifying the best-qualified candidates. The knowledge, skills, abilities, and other characteristics (KSAOs) listed here need to be reinforced as consistently as possible within the scope of the federal resume. Let's review each of these:

(1)   Skill in applying program management concepts.

Relevant skills can include managing programs, organizing events, activities, and operations, and participating in a range of these events. Important elements will include an ability to identify program priorities, organize resources, develop team participation in meeting the organization's objectives, and producing results related to the priorities.

(2)   Skill in coordinating international aviation technical/operational support programs.

The resume needs to demonstrate an understanding of key international aviation technical and operational issues. These can involve anything from airport security when passengers arrive prior to boarding to airport operations to airway facilities design and engineering to air traffic control technology and procedures through arrival controls and international trade, safety, and maintenance considerations at the end of the flight. Few applicants at the GS-13/14 level will be able (or expected) to demonstrate the full range of skills, but the more that can be brought to bear, the better, especially if they coincide with the office's current priorities.

(3)   Skill in coordinating sensitive/complex issues with internal/external organizations.

The resume needs to demonstrate experience working with several other offices within the same organization as well as experience with external organizations. These can include congressional relations, professional associations, other federal agencies with related responsibilities, representatives of other nations, and the media.

(4)   Skill in written communication.

This element is used extensively in evaluating federal applications, especially because major responsibilities of senior officials require abilities to write and present reports. Including a section of major reports completed in previous positions, a list of publications, or similar skills are important. The primary vehicle for assessing an applicant's skill in written communications, however, is the resume itself. No matter how long the list of publications and reports, even a well-presented resume with a significant typographical error will leave reviewers wondering about the level of supervisory skills needed to get the reports done. In this area, an effective resume can overcome any doubts if the previous writing experience is not prominent.

(5)   Skill in oral communication.

This element includes presentations in meetings, participation in group discussions, negotiations, seminars, and a variety of other forums. Regardless of the descriptions on the resume, in practice this skill will be definitively resolved during the course of an interview.

The qualifications listed in this sample announcement are common for transitional positions -- that is, the positions that provide opportunities for people to move senior management from professional series. In technical fields, more specific technical skills will be required. For Senior Executive Service positions, announcements will include three categories of evaluation qualifications: Executive Core Qualifications (five capabilities required of all applicants), Mandatory Technical Qualifications (usually three to five specialized skills) and a set of Desirable Professional Skills (an additional three to five items).

```
NOTE:
   Certain handicapped individuals and disabled veterans eligible
   for special appointing authorities may also apply.
   Ingrade/downgrade applicants will be considered.


NOTE:
   THIS ANNOUNCEMENT MAY BE USED TO FILL OTHER SIMILAR POSITIONS
   SUBJECT TO THE PRIOR APPROVAL OF THE HUMAN RESOURCE MANAGEMENT
   DIVISION.
```

```
NOTE:
    EQUAL OPPORTUNITY THROUGH AFFIRMATIVE ACTION:  The Federal
    Aviation Administration is committed to a multi-cultural
    environment.  Minorities and women are strongly encouraged to
    apply.
```

The notes published with the announcement provide guidance about additional factors that can be considered in evaluating the applications. In this case, the notes emphasize the agency's commitment to "Equal Opportunity Through Affirmative Action," handicapped individuals, and veterans eligible for special appointing authorities. If an applicant qualifies for any of these special consideration factors, the information should be included on the federal resume. Where appropriate, a certificate (such as a DD-214) can be included with the application to confirm eligibility for the special consideration.

```
HOW TO APPLY:
    You may submit a resume, an Application for Federal
    Employment, SF-171 (6/88 or later edition); Optional
    Application  for Federal Employment, OF-612; or any written
    application  that contains the information reflected on the
    attachment entitled "Application Format." NOTE:  If you
    choose to submit the SF-171, you are no longer required to
    complete questions 38-47.  Basic qualifications for the
    position will be determined solely from the information
    included on the application, which must be complete and up-to-
    date.
    On a separate sheet of bond paper, you may provide additional
    information regarding your possession of the KSAOs for this
    position.  (Optional - Not required, however, it provides
    applicants the opportunity to describe portions of their
    experience, training, education, etc., which are directly
    related to the KSAO).  The information will be used for
    ranking of applicants after basic eligibility is determined.
    For each KSAO listed above, provide the following information:
    1) Work Experience: Describe the tasks you have performed
    which demonstrate the KSAO, giving the dates, places, and
    positions where you did this.  2) Education, Training and/or
    Awards: Describe training, education, and/or awards you have
    received which demonstrate the KSA, including the dates you
    received the training, education, and/or awards.  3) Other
    Information:  Such as volunteer experience, hobbies, etc.,
    which demonstrate the KSAO, giving the dates and places where
    you did this.
Supervisory evaluation of KSAs
    Evaluation of Knowledge, Skills and Abilities, completed by
    supervisor (current or former). A completed SF-181, Race and
    National Origin Identification Form.
```

Read these instructions carefully, and follow them to the letter. An application can be rejected for failure to comply with any of them. This announcement indicates that optional application forms (including federal resumes) can be accepted, but they must include all of the information required of people who continue to submit the SF-171.

These instructions include an "option" to submit a statement reflecting each of the

KSAOs on a separate piece of bond paper. The announcement says "optional," but applicants should take advantage of the option. A well-presented set of statements will reinforce all of the qualifications demonstrated on the resume, provide opportunities for expanding on relevant skills, and confirm the writing skills that the position seeks. Well-developed statements can also be invaluable in shaping the interview that will follow a successful resume.

Candidates for Senior Executive Service positions should prepare a solid set of responses to Executive Core Qualifications statements that will be available readily. The Executive Core Qualifications are not automatically described in identical terms, so the applicant should read each phrasing of them carefully to ensure that the standard set is responsive to criteria for each position. A standard set of statements should, however, provide a solid foundation for any modifications made in developing particular vacancy announcements.

```
WHERE TO SEND APPLICATIONS:
    Federal Aviation Administration
    Human Resource Management Division
    Operations Team One, AHR-19A
    800 Independence Avenue, S.W.
    Washington, D.C. 20591
    Applications may be hand-delivered to Room 109.

    All applications must be received by the closing date of this
    announcement.
    Please call (202) 267-8007 for additional information.
```

This item informs people of where they must be addressed or delivered. Remember that agencies always have the discretion to reject applications transmitted through interoffice mail. Proper postage, or personal delivery of the application in a personal envelope, will resolve any concerns about this factor. (See the final item under "Excepted Service" on the announcement.)

```
Excepted Service:
    On April 1, 1996 the Federal Aviation Administration (FAA)
    created a new personnel system, the Federal Aviation Service
    (FAS). The FAS excepts the FAA from most traditional Federal
    personnel laws. Basic Federal employee benefits like
    retirement, health and life insurance, workers' compensation,
    and holidays will remain the same for FAA employees as for
    other Federal employees. Present Federal employees currently
    occupying positions in the Competitive Service will, if
    selected for FAA positions, be converted to the Excepted
    Service under the FAS. Current leave balances and other
    benefits will be transferred to the FAA.
    Privacy Act Requirements (P.L. 93-579): The referenced forms
    are used to determine qualifications for promotional and
    career opportunities, and are authorized under Title 5 of U.S.
    Code, Sections 3302 and 3361.
    Each specified form must be submitted in order for you to be
    considered for promotion to the position being advertised.
    The social security number is not required for this purpose
    and may be deleted from the forms submitted. The servicing
```

```
human resource management office of the office named in this
announcement will be able to provide information on Specific
Privacy Act requirements.
DOT is an equal opportunity employer.  Selections shall be
made regardless of race, color, religion, national origin,
sex, age, physical and/or mental handicap, marital or parental
status, political or employee organizational affiliation.
Applicants who fail to submit required forms will not be
considered.  Forms requiring signature and date may be
reproduced, but must be submitted with original signatures and
dates to be accepted.  Send only those forms required.  None
of these forms will be subsequently loaned or returned to the
applicant.
Use of postage-paid Government envelopes to file job
applications is a violation of Federal laws and regulations.
Applications submitted in postage-paid Government envelopes
will not be considered.
```
FAA vacancy information and certain application forms are now
available on the FAA's World Wide Web site at:
http://jobs.faa.gov or by calling our Faxback system at (405)954-
0250.

This section describes the unique current status of the Federal Aviation Administration, which gained authority to initiate its own personnel system. The excepted service is likely to expand considerably in the coming years, whether through the Administration's program to move toward "Performance Based Organizations," or expanded authority to conduct "demonstration projects" that the Office of Personnel Management can approve or Congress can authorize.

This section contains several additional details about the application that must be included in preparation. Note, applicants can omit their social security numbers, but they must provide documents with original signatures and dates. Do not get rejected by submitting a photocopy (it might even be best to sign the original in blue to make certain that the original can be distinguished from the photocopies that will be made in the personnel office).

Having covered the announcement and application process, let's turn to an example of the modification process necessary to turn your federal resume into a successful application.

Reinvention KSA Writing Tips

Vice President Gore's Blair House Papers include reinvention success stories by federal employees that resulted in responsiveness to customers' needs, saving the government money, saving time, increasing efficiency and improving overall performance. These stories can become an important accomplishment for a federal resume and a KSA statement. Also included in a good KSA can be a relevant college degree, professional courses, certifications, volunteer activities, awards or honors that support the particular KSA statement.

KSA success stories are written in plain English, but include specific skills and language of the position (which are excellent for getting "hits" from scanning.

The Blair House success stories and KSAs include 6 elements:

KSA Success Story Elements:
What your role is (title of job, agency).
What you do (use verbiage from the KSA statement)
What the situation or problem was.
What you did to change it.
How you changed it and who was affected.
What the result is/was.

Examples of Blair House KSAs are at the Federal Resume Writing Website: http://www.resume-place.com/jobs

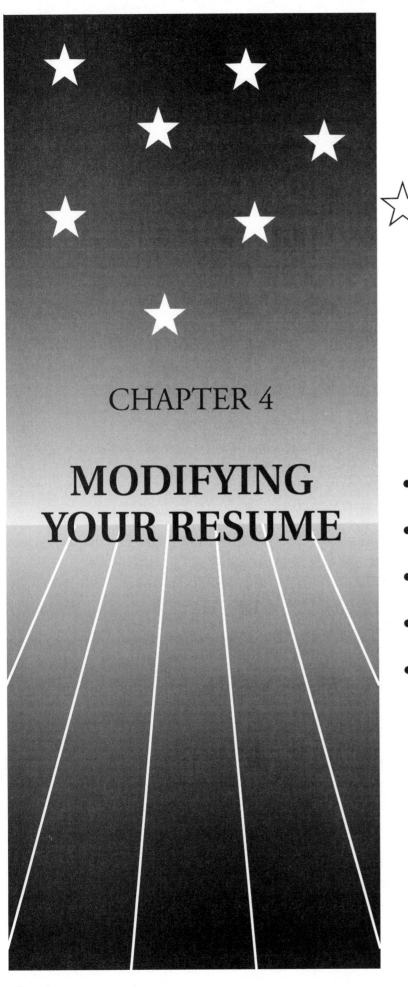

CHAPTER 4

MODIFYING YOUR RESUME

- Case Study

- *Before*

- *After*

- KSAs

- Covering Letter

Modifying Your Resume to Fit the Position

A Working Example of a Successful Transitional Senior Management Resume

The resume (*after*) presented on the next page is a modification of one submitted by a client (*before*), with names, actual locations, and other identifying features modified substantially. The applicant wants to make a career change, and the resume will be modified to provide illustrations of the background and experience that would make the applicant a suitable candidate for this position -- a position that closely resembles the objective intended as career transition plans were developed.

First, let's review the *before* resume in terms of the core qualifications, and examine its strengths and weaknesses.

(1) *Skill in applying program management concepts.*

The resume shows some recent experience (in the developmental assignment) that could fit under these qualifications, but the accomplishments that fit well in this category are thin. More, the profile claims some experience under this qualification factor, but it is not supported effectively in any of the job blocks on the federal resume. This is a critical shortcoming -- especially because some of the applicant's awards indicate several successes in these areas.

(2) *Skill in coordinating international aviation technical/operational support programs.*

Although the applicant has been with the Federal Aviation Administration for several years, the work described on the resume shows little "international aviation technical/operational support programs" experience.

(3) *Skill in coordinating sensitive/complex issues with internal/ external organizations.*

The resume accurately reflects relevant skills in public affairs activities that require coordination with internal/external organizations. These, as we will see, can be described in ways that serve the candidate better.

(4) _Skill in written communication._

Qualifications in this area are outstanding, for the most part. Again, however, the skill in written communication needs to be used to reinforce awareness of the aviation operations issues related to this region of the world.

(5) _Skill in oral communication._

Again, the resume indicates strong oral communications skills, and the application will demonstrate a strong ability to conduct interviews and meetings.

What Is Missing?

Parentheses refer to specific cites in the **before** (b) and **after** (a) resumes.

17 year Gap in Dates

First, the **before** resume shows a seventeen year gap between college graduation (1971) and the first professional experience listed. Even though the "Honors & Awards" at the end of the resume show awards for film production during the 1970s, they do not appear linked to any job. The federal resume should show relevant professional experience for at least ten years, especially for a senior position. If people have been enrolled in graduate or professional school during that period, the enrollment should be shown, even if it did not lead to a degree or certificate. This resume shows extensive professional development training; if any of that would fill in the 17-year gap, dates could be shown with the training.

Filling in the Gaps with Training, Education, Volunteer, Fundraising Activities

People returning to work after caring for families, (usually raising children), must make special effort to demonstrate that college skills were sustained -- or augmented -- during such a gap. This is especially important for people who are considering a career shift, or seeking positions well above the entry level. Volunteer work (especially leadership) can be described in terms of relevant responsibilities. Also, fundraising activities, or program management of volunteer projects can fill such gaps.

More Emphasis on Operations and Technical Qualifications

Second, and perhaps most significant, the current presentation of the *before* resume shows little in the way of familiarity with either aviation program operations or issues or with Asian nations, history, or culture.

Other resume examples included in the back section of this workbook show greater surface experience in international trade issues that could become relevant for this position. Experience compiling a history of a military reunion of Pearl Harbor veterans can show the applicant's interest in the region, but doesn't begin to touch the technical qualifications. Although program and budgeting experience is claimed in the profile, no subsequent position description corroborates the claim.

Using a Developmental Assignment to Increase Technical Qualifications

The candidate needs to address these concerns to get the resume into position for serious consideration. First, in a situation such as this, it is important that the applicant use recent developmental assignments to strengthen qualifications for such a position. In doing this, it would be helpful, for example, if the applicant could describe parts of the assignments that looked like preparation for such a position. An ideal assignment for such a position, for example, might be to serve as a meeting facilitator on international agreements related to maintenance treaties with the governments in the region. The work with the Customs Service, for another example, might include participation in discussions related to the exchange of passengers and merchandise between governments in the region.

Organize and Target the Training List

Third, the professional training listed in this resume is not focused on the credentials that are relevant to this position. An interest in Asian affairs, for example, might be better reflected by a course in Chinese or Hindi, rather than Russian. The extensive list of courses is very strong in the communications area, and relatively strong on recent management themes, but totally lacking in the technical/program area. If this training is recent (and it is not dated in the first version) it would appear that it is not oriented toward the objective of this announcement.

Strengthening Measures Developed During Preparation for Career Transition

Many of the strengthening measures would have to be developed during preparation to write the resume. The applicant should select training with an appropriate job objective in mind. Rather than building upon strengths, training should be used to fill gaps. Some training (for example, in diversity) is mandatory in a variety of agencies. More than one or two courses in such a field, however, might leave a rating official with the impression that the applicant is more interested in career advancement in the equal employment opportunity counseling field than in a technical area.

Clearly Present Writing Skills

In addition, an employee who is obviously a skilled writer and presenter should select topics that will advance such an objective. In writing for the agency magazine (*FAA World*), the author should submit manuscripts that report on programs related to potential advancement. One article demonstrating familiarity -- for example -- with satellite air traffic control technology for the Pacific region could take a major step toward reflecting the program familiarity that reviewers will seek.

Improve Statement of Results, not Functional Descriptions

For all of the employee's writing skills, however, the position descriptions in the first version of the resume show little evidence of quantification or results. They are functional descriptions rather than results-oriented, and that transformation can make a real difference to the person reading the resume.

Presentation and Organization

In contrasting the two examples, the author has taken the liberty of strengthening the background, and reorganizing the presentation style. Rather than chronological order, for example, education is presented in reverse chronological order. Training is reorganized in terms of its relevance to the position sought, and without regard for chronological order. The revised resume omits training that is not relevant to the announced vacancy, and adds courses that support the application. The second resume adds experience that will take the applicant back another two years -- to cover the ten years required on federal resumes. And, adding free-lance writing experience, the talents can be logically connected to the applicant's subsequent professional development.

"Before"

ROBERTA E. SPENCER
124 3rd Street, NE,
Washington, DC 20002

Home: (202) 567-8910	Work: (202) 267-9976

Social Security Number: 345-87-6540   *Veteran's Status*: N/A
Federal Civilian Status: Public Affairs Specialist, GS-12   *Citizenship*: U.S.

OBJECTIVE: International Aviation Operations Specialist, AWA-AIA-96-1379-10590

PROFILE:

Communications specialist with over 15 years experience demonstrating organizational skills, award-winning literary products, and development and maintenance of positive interpersonal relationships among government employees, industry representatives, and academia. Adept at reviewing, analyzing, monitoring, and maintaining government and private industry programs, budgets, and collateral materials which have organization-wide impact. Skilled in writing, speaking, designing and organizing programs that educate both internal and external customers on the agency mission and activities.

PROFESSIONAL EXPERIENCE:

FEDERAL AVIATION ADMINISTRATION   October 1991 to Present
800 Independence Avenue, SW   40 hrs./week
Washington, DC 20591   Starting Salary: $35,136
Supervisor: Roger Sperrin (202) 267-9975   Current Salary: $47,154
You may contact present employer

Deputy Public Affairs Officer, GS-12/4   October 1993 to Present

Fulfill all the responsibilities of the official spokesperson for the FAA Headquarters in the absence of the Public Affairs Officer. Provide the public, using the news media as the principal intermediary, with information about the agency's mission, policies, and operations.

Due to a shortage of personnel, I conducted a month-long detail in FAA's Office of Public Affairs in Los Angeles, CA, during which I assumed all responsibilities of the Public Affairs Officer in the second largest media market in the United States.

Conceptualize, formulate, develop, and conduct public affairs campaigns to enhance the understanding of FAA programs among the general public, specialized groups and organizations, and FAA employees. This involves the design, writing, and final layout of copy for internal and external agency brochures and ad campaigns.

Provide aviation writers, newspaper representatives, feature writers, and free-lance reporters with stories, background material and first-hand experience through visits to agency facilities to enable them to develop accurate news and feature material for public release.

Evaluate information, identify existing or potential issues and submit proposals to members of the Regional Management Team for review and/or approval.

"After"

ROBERTA E. SPENCER
124 3rd Street, NE,
Washington, DC 20002

| Home: (202) 567-8910 | Work: (202) 267-9976 |

Social Security Number: 345-87-6540
Federal Civilian Status: Public Affairs Specialist, GS-12

Veteran's Status: N/A
Citizenship: U.S.

OBJECTIVE: International Aviation Operations Specialist, AWA-AIA-96-1379-10590

PROFILE: Aviation communications professional with over 15 years experience demonstrating organizational skills, award-winning media relations, and development and maintenance of positive relationships among government employees, industry representatives, and academia. Recent assignments include special project involving Pacific region air transportation technology and multiple agency missions. Adept at reviewing, analyzing, and maintaining government and private industry programs, budgets, and collateral materials with international effects.

RECENT ACCOMPLISHMENTS

- Facilitated international meetings of Chinese, Filipino, Indian, and Pakistani media briefings after negotiations of air traffic control protocols for Pacific Ocean flights. Prepared briefing materials and agendas, organized presentations, and ensured complete media access to technical officials. Presentations resulted in major international coverage for innovative technologies in air commerce.

- Completed developmental assignment with U.S. Customs Service to publicize strengthened enforcement of smuggling laws with regard to major Asian nations. Coordinated presentations for international meetings involving Maylasian, Pakistani, and Filipino governments and presenting resolution of complex international negotiations.

- Published articles in **FAA World** describing agency perspective on success of international negotiations. Reported advances in air traffic control technology, new agreement with the Peoples' Republic of China for maintenance of aircraft consistent with FAA standards, and new international smuggling accord.

PROFESSIONAL EXPERIENCE:

FEDERAL AVIATION ADMINISTRATION
800 Independence Avenue, SW
Washington, DC 20591
Supervisor: Roger Sperrin (202) 267-9975
You may contact present employer

October 1991 to Present
40 hrs./week
Starting Salary: $35,136
Current Salary: $47,154

Deputy Public Affairs Officer, GS-12/4

October 1993 to Present

Represent FAA Headquarters before general media in the absence of the Public Affairs Officer. Coordinated seven-person branch providing public information about the agency's mission, policies, and operations to ensure timely and responsive presentation of sensitive issues of aviation policy and technology. Earned recognition from print and electronic media for professionalism of briefings and quick responses to technical topics.

Managed month-long detail in FAA's Los Angeles Public Affairs Office to provide major market coverage of sensitive issues involving U.S. agencies and Asian-Pacific nations. Achieved substantial public awareness of impact of new trade agreements on international transportation systems.

"Before"

Public Affairs Specialist, GS-11/12   October 1991 - 1993
FAA Aviation Education Program Manager

Editor of weekly employee newsletter electronically disseminated to 2,735 Washington area FAA employees. Established systematic procedures to solicit reader input and produce a cost-effective product that kept employees knowledgeable about agency issues and programs.

Promoted and encouraged partnerships with businesses, education, and government organizations involving aviation activities. These efforts contributed to further development of a multi-agency commitment to the aviation education program that impacted several thousand students each year.

Developed and implemented budgetary requirements and procedures for media campaigns; determined annual calendar of events for the Public Affairs Office; and devised and implemented components and timelines for FAA's Aviation Education program that impacted thousands of students throughout the Mid-Atlantic region by creating awareness of career opportunities for future aviation professionals.

Frequently addressed various educational groups at colleges, universities, and seminars to promote an understanding of the agency and its programs and objectives.

Conducted numerous investigative interviews with employees and members of the media and public to ascertain appropriate information to be noted in print at a later time.

PREVIOUS EXPERIENCE:

DEPARTMENT OF DEFENSE   October 1988 - 1991
Pacific Air Command   40 hrs./week
The Pentagon, Washington, DC 20330   Starting Salary: $28,997
Supervisor: Rod Serling (202) 737-8637   Ending Salary: $34,136

Assistant Command Historian, GS-9

Worked with a three-person team to conduct in-depth interviews of military leaders at Air Force Bases for annual historical records that are maintained under classified conditions. These histories averaged 800 pages in length with an equal number of pages of supporting documents.

Upon request from the Commanding General at a major USAF command, I designed and managed the construction of two exhibits for the foyer in Command Headquarters that averaged 50 square-feet in size and included historical information on the military in Hawaii in a compatible environment with local wildlife displays.

Coordinated a reunion of over 100 veterans from the 11th Air Force who fought in Hawaii during World War II. The event included three days of activities on Pearl Harbor Naval Station that highlighted a 45-minute video featuring many of the attendees in actual film footage from the war. I organized their lodging, meals, transportation needs, and conducted exit interviews before they departed Hawaii.

"After"

FAA (continued):

Public Affairs Specialist, GS-1035-11/12
FAA Aviation Education Program Manager
Supervisor: William Leytle (202) 267-8338

October 1991 - 1993
40 hrs./week
Starting Salary: $29,876
Ending Salary: $31,352

Edited weekly employee newsletter electronically disseminated to 2,735 Washington-area FAA employees. Established systematic procedures to solicit reader input and produce a cost-effective product that kept employees knowledgeable about agency issues and programs. Innovations in on-line production technology cut distribution time by one-third while realizing 20 percent cost savings.

Promoted and encouraged partnerships with businesses, education, and government organizations involving aviation activities. Enhanced development of a multi-agency commitment to the aviation education program that reached several thousand students each year. New pilot licensing in Headquarters region increased 7 percent annually during this program.

Developed and implemented budgetary requirements and procedures for media campaigns. Scheduled annual calendar for the Public Affairs Office. Devised and implemented components and timelines for strengthened general aviation safety concepts in FAA's Aviation Education program. Campaign cited by AOPA for reducing general aviation accident rate during 1993.

Conducted investigative interviews with employees and members of the media to provide technical background related to revised air traffic control procedures resulting from new airport radar systems at metropolitan Washington airports.

PREVIOUS EXPERIENCE:

DEPARTMENT OF DEFENSE
Pacific Air Command
The Pentagon, Washington, DC 20330
Supervisor: Rod Serling (202) 737-8637

October 1988 - 1991
40 hrs./week
Starting Salary: $24,865
Ending Salary: $27,546

Assistant Command Historian, GS-9

Coordinated three-member team conducting interviews with military leaders at Air Force Bases for annual historical records maintained under classified conditions. These histories averaged 800 pages in length with an equal number of pages of supporting documents. Secured and monitored publication contracts for multi-volume editions.

Designed and managed construction of two foyer exhibits for Command Headquarters. Identified key command achievements over a fifty year period; researched print and photo archives to ensure accuracy and attractiveness of presentation. Exhibits averaged 50 square-feet and included historical information on the military in Hawaii in a compatible environment with local wildlife displays.

Organized 50th anniversary reunion of more than 100 veterans from the 11th Air Force who fought in Hawaii during World War II. The event included three days of activities on Pearl Harbor Naval Station and highlighted a 45-minute video featuring many of the attendees in vintage film footage. Arranged lodging, meals, and transportation, and conducted exit interviews with 80 percent of participants before departure. Convention cited by Air Force Association Historical Society.

"Before"

EDUCATION & TRAINING:

Diploma *Robert Fulton High School* June 1967
Queens, New York 10065

Associate of Arts · · · · · · *Simi Valley Community College* · · · · · June 1969
Los Angeles, CA 95701

Bachelor of Arts · · · · · · · *University of California-Los Angeles* · · June 1971
Los Angeles, CA 95701
(Speech & Communications)

PROFESSIONAL DEVELOPMENT/TRAINING:

U.S.D.A. Graduate School · 1995-1996
Aviation Executive Leadership Program
Mentor: Charlene Derry (907) 271-5534
Successfully completed developmental assignments emphasizing leadership and management potential as Assistant to FAA's International Liaison Officer for 60 days and as Assistant to the Resident Agent-in-Charge with the U.S. Customs Office for 30 days. The formalized classroom training with the program included more than five weeks of coursework involving leadership styles, managing conflict, empowerment, stress management, and cultural diversity management. Intensive cluster group assignments addressed challenges of performance management in a team environment.

Other Professional Courses:

Thinking Beyond the Boundaries	Hawaii Press Women
Managing Public Communication	FAA Center for Management Development
Management Skills for Non-Supervisors	Discovering Diversity and Valuing the Diverse Workforce
Career Planning and Development	Seven Habits of Highly Effective People
Conversational Russian I	Public Involvement Training
The Quality Advantage	Collateral Duty Recruiter Training
Constructive Communications	Communications Training Workshop
Investment in Excellence	Introduction to Emergency Readiness
ZAP Production Costs,	Oral Listening and Archives Workshop
Proofreading and Basic Skills Improvement	Detail, FAA Civil Aviation Security Office (2 wks)

"After"

DOD: (continued)

Research Historian   September, 1985 - 1988
Hawaii Naval Air Station, Honolulu, HI   40 hrs./week
Supervisor: Mr. John Clayton (808) 546-7785   Starting Salary: $21,156
                                                            Ending Salary: $23,652

Reviewed development and implementation of air transportation systems supporting Allied Pacific operations during World War II. Historical research developed full documentation of aircraft, airport, and airway support technologies and procedures used to integrate multinational air, sea, and land forces.

Defined resource requirements to support development of oral history and film presentations to support expansion of Base history project. Supported production of video material from Army and Navy Archives.

Published more than four significant historical articles per year based on research. Coordinated meetings of local historical association and negotiated command support for multi-media presentations.

EDUCATION & TRAINING:

Bachelor of Arts (Speech & Communications)	*University of California-Los Angeles* Los Angeles, CA 95701	June 1971
Associate of Arts	*Simi Valley Community* Los Angeles, CA 95701	June 1969
Diploma	*Robert Fulton High School* Queens, NY 10065	June 1967

PROFESSIONAL DEVELOPMENT/TRAINING:

U.S.D.A. Graduate School   1995-1996
Aviation Executive Leadership Program
Mentor: Charlene Derry (907) 271-5534
Successfully completed developmental assignments emphasizing leadership and management potential. Formalized classroom training included leadership styles, managing conflict, empowerment, stress, and cultural diversity management. Cluster group assignments focused on improving performance management in a team environment.

- Assistant to FAA's International Liaison Officer for 60 days in planning and performance of multi-national meetings developing protocols to shift air traffic control technology over Pacific Ocean routes. Coordinated media presence in three-day international meetings, securing substantial favorable coverage for the U.S. government and the agency.

- Assisted the Resident Agent-in-Charge with the U.S. Customs Office for 30 days. Managed public affairs for international smuggling conference, providing important coverage for new international law enforcement protocols governing movement of passengers and freight. Supported operation through media expertise and technical familiarity with airspace system operations.

"Before"

PROFESSIONAL PUBLICATIONS:

    Co-author, "Woman & Minorities in Aviation in Hawaii," Hawaii Office of Education, 1994.
    Article in FAA World, a national monthly newsletter to all FAA employees nationwide.
    Article in Aviation Education News, a national quarterly newsletter to all FAA employees.
    Author, "Our Hawaii," marketing book used worldwide by private corporation in Hawaii.

CONFERENCES ATTENDED:

    Hawaii Conference on Women and Minorities
    National Congress on Aviation & Space Education
    Civil Air Patrol Commanders' Call Conference
    National Association of Travel Agents

PROFESSIONAL MEMBERSHIPS & AFFILIATIONS:

    Civil Air Patrol, Director of Aerospace Education for State of Hawaii
    Federal Women's Program
    Air Traffic Advisory Committee, University of Hawaii - Kauai
    Hawaii Aerospace Development Corporation
    Summer Surf Tournament Committee
    Barber Shop Quartet Society of Hawaii
    Boy Scouts of America
    American Heart Association
    Elected to local Parish Council
    Air Force Association
    Honolulu Chamber of Commerce

HONORS & AWARDS:

1995	National Award for Excellence in Aerospace Education from Civil Air Patrol (Brewer Award)
1995	Participant in Aviation Executive Leadership Program
1994	Special Recognition Award from Kauai Council of Girl Scouts in Honolulu, Hawaii
1993	FAA Employee of the Year Award (Category III, GS-12 and above)
1993	Certificate of Achievement from Federal Executive Association
1992	Chuck Yeager Regional Award for Excellence in Aerospace Education from Civil Air Patrol
1987	Award of Notable Achievement, DoD (for producing displays for General Graham)
1983	Public Relations Society Association Award (for corporate newsletter)
1979	International Film Festival Award (for production of educational film)
1977	National Pacesetter Award (for California Office of Education publication)

"After"

Other Professional Courses
Aviation Technical Courses:
Detail, FAA Civil Aviation Security Office (1995)
Introduction to Emergency Readiness (1995)
Air Traffic Control History (1994)
Managing Public Communication, FAA Center for Management Development (1993)

Management Development Courses: (All 1994)
Seven Habits of Highly Effective People   The Quality Advantage
Management Skills for Non-Supervisors   Investment in Excellence
Discovering Diversity/Valuing the Diverse Workforce   Thinking Beyond the Boundaries

Communications Training:
Public Involvement Training (1991)
Collateral Duty Recruiter Training (1990)
Constructive Communications (1988)
Communications Training Workshop (1989)

RECENT PROFESSIONAL PUBLICATIONS:

Co-author, **Woman & Minorities in Aviation in Hawaii,** Hawaii Office of Education, 1994
"Aviation Progress in the Pacific," **FAA World**, October 1995
"Safety Basics for the Novice Pilot," **Aviation Education News**, Fall 1993
Our Hawaii, marketing book used worldwide by private corporation in Hawaii, 1988
The Air War in the Pacific, (Honolulu, Air Force Historical Association), 1987

CONFERENCES ATTENDED:

Hawaii Conference on Women and Minorities
National Congress on Aviation & Space Education
Civil Air Patrol Commanders' Call Conference
National Association of Travel Agents

PROFESSIONAL MEMBERSHIPS & AFFILIATIONS:

Air Traffic Advisory Committee
Air Force Association
Hawaii Aerospace Development Corporation
Federal Women's Program
Civil Air Patrol Aviation Education and Professional Development Committee
Honolulu Chamber of Commerce

HONORS & AWARDS:

Outstanding Performance Ratings seven consecutive years	1989 - 1995
National Award for Excellence in Aerospace Education from Civil Air Patrol (Brewer Award)	1995
Participant in Women's Executive Leadership (WEL) Program	1995
Special Recognition Award from Kauai Council of Girl Scouts in Honolulu, Hawaii	1994
FAA Employee of the Year Award (Category III, GS-12 and above)	1993
Certificate of Achievement from Federal Executive Association	1993
Chuck Yeager Regional Award for Excellence in Aerospace Education from Civil Air Patrol	1992
Award of Notable Achievement, Dept. Of Defense (for Completion of History Program)	1987
Public Relations Society Association Award (for corporate newsletter)	1983
International Film Festival Award (for production of educational film)	1979
National Pacesetter Award (for California Office of Education publication)	1977

DEPARTMENT OF TRANSPORTATION
Federal Aviation Administration

Position: International Aviation Operations Specialist, GS-0301-13/14
Announcement No. AWA-AIA-96-1379-10590

ROBERTA E. SPENCER
SS# 345-87-6540

KNOWLEDGE, SKILLS, AND ABILITIES

(1)   Skill in applying program management concepts.

My career reflects more than fifteen years of progressively responsible experience in both public and private sector positions requiring communications management positions. I have supervised the development and implementation of national media strategies to support the FAA's safety and air commerce regulatory initiatives. I have supervised seven people in my current position, and coordinated the work of task forces involving as many as thirty people representing both diverse federal agencies and different nations. My experience includes responsibility for the development and defense of program budgets during the agency's annual budget cycle. I earned recognition from the Aircraft Owners and Pilots Association (AOPA) for approaches to aviation education that increased pilot registration by 7 percent in a single year. I also received a letter of commendation from the U.S. Customs Service for designing a publicity campaign that assisted their efforts to reduce airborne smuggling from Asian airports.

I recently completed a developmental program that expanded my familiarity with customer-oriented management techniques, and found this approach helpful in contributing to the public affairs portion of the FAA's strategic plan. My bachelor's degree, earned at UCLA, included courses on managing communications organizations. As reflected on my federal resume, my continuing professional training incorporates a balance of the technical training and managerial concepts intended to prepare me for changes in management principles associated with the reinvention of government and emerging federal management laws and procedures.

(2)   Skill in coordinating international aviation technical/operational support programs.

My recent developmental assignments and professional education reflect my commitment that technical knowledge is critical to effective communications. I developed a thorough understanding of the air traffic control system and civil aviation security procedures through professional training. I have also developed, through work experiences, knowledge of international airway systems and the communications technologies needed to support the shift from land-based to satellite-based air traffic control being planned by FAA and international aviation leadership. My communications work has enabled me to provide substantive support to the U.S. Customs Service in developing tactics to reduce airborne international smuggling, as well as enabled me to facilitate multinational meetings on the topics. As reflected on my federal resume, I first gained knowledge of international air traffic operations through work at the Department of Defense. I studied the long-term conversion of international air traffic control systems in preparation for my current experiences. This technical knowledge has served me well in my current position, and prepared me for managerial responsibilities in the area.

(3)   Skill in coordinating sensitive/complex issues with internal/external organizations.

During the past ten years, I have worked closely with technical aviation organizations, both U.S. and international media, and agencies of the U.S. and other national governments. This series of active professional relations is complemented by an extensive network of professional memberships that contribute to my technical knowledge of aviation programs (for example, membership on the Air Traffic Advisory Committee) and have also provided experiences in community development and perspectives on the management of other agencies and government. This series of associations has enabled me to anticipate concerns that are likely to develop in the course of issuing major regulations in the U.S., and to be attentive to concerns of other governments, who are substantially influenced by the leadership that the FAA provides in international aviation. Although I have addressed controversial issues during much of my tenure, my work has gained professional and community recognition, from other government agencies, from interest groups active in FAA's policy areas, from professional associations, and community organizations. These awards reflect a consistent ability to work with other people and build consensus for the implementation of effective policies. These skills are essential qualifications for the advertised position.

(4)   Skill in written communications.

My current responsibilities require preparation of briefing materials, speeches, legislative testimony, and media advisories on a recurring basis. My ability to write quickly and accurately about technical topics has earned consistent praise in performance evaluations. It has also assisted in facilitating complex negotiations involving other U.S. government agencies and both governmental and nongovernmental organizations of other nations. In addition to the frequent writing required by my current position, I have published several articles that expand on my official duties. Several of these articles have contributed to my efforts to provide additional information about agency initiatives through internal communications channels, thus broadening the information available to all agency employees. This combination of professional and independent publications reflects the timely and precise writing skills essential for this position.

(5)   Skill in oral communications.

My oral communications skills are well respected within the agency and among the professional associations where I have presented papers and speeches. In supervising a staff of seven, I frequently provide oral guidance related to projects under short deadlines. I consistently provide clear instructions, and identify appropriate contacts to provide technical support. My duties involve frequent meetings with senior agency leadership, and I am able to participate actively in key discussions that shape agency strategy. I regularly conduct phone briefings of media representatives, and the coverage that I have gained is accurate and incorporates solid understanding of technical regulations. As reflected on my federal resume, my experience also includes facilitating international negotiations on technical matters, responsibilities that have resulted in significant operational improvements and publicity that have served the FAA well. I have appeared on camera when necessary, and am comfortable conducting meetings essential to all functions that would fall within the responsibilities of this position.

ROBERTA E. SPENCER
124 3rd Street, NE
Washington, DC 20002

Date

Director, Operations Team One, AHR-19A
Human Resource Management Division
Federal Aviation Administration
800 Independence Avenue, SW
Washington, DC 20591

Dear Operations Team One Manager:

This letter transmits my application for the International Aviation Operations Specialist, GS-0301-13/14, position announced by your agency. I would appreciate your full consideration for the position. Let me describe the enclosed documentation that supports this application.

My credentials are summarized in a federal resume that contains information consistent with OPM criteria. I am currently a federal employee with ten years' experience, including positions with both the Department of Defense and the FAA, that provide program management experience and an understanding of aviation technology. My current position has afforded me opportunities to represent the agency in major air commerce and international regulatory activities. This experience demonstrates well the managerial and technical qualifications essential for this position.

I have also included statements summarizing my experiences and training related to each of the ranking factors identified as selection criteria. My most recent positions have relied upon program management skills, and I recently completed a developmental assignment that complemented my supervisory experience. This assignment highlighted my abilities to deal with sensitive and complex issues in an environment that included interagency and international factors. My knowledge of airspace system technology has increased in each of my positions. I have displayed excellent oral and written communications skills in extensive dealings with print and electronic media.

I can be reached at the phone numbers on the resume if you have any questions. Thank you for your consideration. I look forward to this opportunity, and believe that this combination of experience and training make me an especially suitable candidate to meet the agency's needs.

Sincerely,

Roberta E. Spencer

Enclosures

One-Page "Calling-Card" Resume

Networking and Self-Marketing Tool

The resume presented on the next page is a one-page version of Roberta Spencer's four-page federal resume. A one-page resume is a very subtle selling document. In just 10 to 15 seconds the reader can scan your job titles, employers, dates, education, publications and awards – believe it or not! Informing others of your background and capabilities is a smart method of pre-marketing for task forces, teams, career development programs, promotions and could position you for an upcoming new career opportunity. You might believe your supervisor or co-worker knows your background, but they really don't know the full extent of your experience. Hand them the one-page resume and they can keep in it in a file for future consideration.

> *Roberta Spencer could have used this type of resume in the following situations:*
> ♦ As an application for the Detail to the FAA Civil Aviation Security Office.
> ♦ As an application for the Career Development Program, the two Details, to recruit a mentor, or to entice senior managers into giving her interview time.
> ♦ As a Biography or Introduction for publication submissions, speech introductions, and for her award presentations.

"OF-510 Compliance Details" are Missing

This one-page resume does not contain any of the compliance details of the federal resume because this is not the resume you would use to apply for a job in response to a vacancy announcement. The reader does not need to know your supervisor's name, Social Security number, citizenship or other details until there is a serious interest in a job. This resume is simply an outline of your entire background, touching on skills, education, places of employment, and includes a profile statement summarizing career highlights.

Editing and Content Selection for the One-Page Presentation

Profile: Answers the question: "Tell me about yourself," sets the tone of the resume; highlights the major strengths and experience.

Professional Experience: A simple outline: titles, employers, dates; this section does not describe her responsibilities because the *Honors & Awards* section states that her work has been outstanding. The reader will have to meet with Roberta to get more information on the job responsibilities.

Education & Training: Significant courses and programs.

Publications: Important for Roberta because she is in public affairs.

Professional Presentations: Highlights communications skills.

Honors & Awards: Important section, since she received many awards and recognitions for outstanding work experience.

One Page "Calling-Card" Resume for Networking

ROBERTA E. SPENCER
124 3rd Street, NE,
Washington, DC 20002

Home: (202) 567-8910   Work: (202) 267-9976

PROFILE: **Aviation communications professional** with over 15 years experience demonstrating organizational skills, award-winning media relations, and development and maintenance of positive relationships among government employees, industry representatives, and academia. Recent assignments include special project involving Pacific region air transportation technology and multiple agency missions. Adept at reviewing, analyzing, and maintaining government and private industry programs, budgets, and collateral materials with international effects.

PROFESSIONAL EXPERIENCE:

Deputy Public Affairs Officer, GS-12/4   1993 - Present
Federal Aviation Administration, Washington, DC
♦   Detail, FAA Civil Aviation Security Office (1995)

Public Affairs Specialist, GS-1035-11/12   1991 - 1993
♦   *FAA Aviation Education Program Manager*

Assistant Command Historian, GS-9
Department of Defense, The Pentagon, Washington, DC   1988 - 1991

EDUCATION & TRAINING:

B.A., Speech & Communications, University of California-Los Angeles

U.S.D.A. Graduate School, Aviation Executive Leadership Program, 1995-1996
•   Assistant to FAA's International Liaison Officer for 60 days.
•   Assisted the Resident Agent-in-Charge with the U.S. Customs Office for 30 days.

PUBLICATIONS:

Co-author, ***Woman & Minorities in Aviation in Hawaii,*** Hawaii Office of Education   1994
"Aviation Progress in the Pacific," ***FAA World***   October, 1995
"Safety Basics for the Novice Pilot," ***Aviation Education News***   Fall, 1993
Our Hawaii, marketing book used worldwide by private corporation in Hawaii   1988
The Air War in the Pacific, (Honolulu, Air Force Historical Association)   1987

PROFESSIONAL PRESENTATIONS:

Hawaii Conference on Women and Minorities, National Congress on Aviation & Space Education
Civil Air Patrol Commanders' Call Conference, National Association of Travel Agents

HONORS & AWARDS:

Outstanding Performance Ratings seven consecutive years   1989 - 1995
National Award for Excellence in Aerospace Education from Civil Air Patrol (Brewer Award)1995
Special Recognition Award from Kauai Council of Girl Scouts in Honolulu, Hawaii   1994
FAA Employee of the Year Award (Category III, GS-12 and above)   1993
Chuck Yeager Regional Award for Excellence in Aerospace Education from Civil Air Patrol 1992
Award of Notable Achievement, Dept. Of Defense (**for *Completion of History Program*)   1987
Public Relations Society Association Award (for *corporate newsletter*)

CHAPTER 5

WRITING A SCANNABLE FEDERAL RESUME

- Critical Skills

- Maximizing Hits

- Format and Content

- E-Mail Format

Writing a Scannable Federal Resume

Many large companies use computer generated software to scan resumes to identify the candidates who will be considered for interviews. Federal agencies appear to be following -- in one leap -- from the paper intensive SF-171 to the electronically-transmitted Federal Resume. Each resume scanning program has unique instructions. Computer scanning of resumes reduces opportunities for people to act independently. The good news is that this can nearly eliminate the importance of "who you know" while increasing the importance of the qualifications on your resume. Because the resume is much more important in a scanning system, it is essential to understand what the new system requires. And, the first requirement of any successful application is to read the instructions carefully for any system, and follow them to the letter.

What is a Scannable Federal Resume?

A scannable federal resume is a resume that describes your qualifications in a way that allows them to be read and analyzed by a computer. The computer is programmed in a sophisticated manner that enables it to sort through the context of what you put into the document. If you use the letters ADA, for example, the machine is programmed to distinguish, from the context, whether you mean Americans with Disabilities Act, American Dental Association, or Ada, Oklahoma. In preparing your federal resume, knowing how the machine is programmed is essential in knowing what to write.

(1)   Understand the format.

In providing instructions for submitting a federal resume, agencies provide distinct instructions for transmitting by e-mail, fax, or regular mail. Presentation makes a difference no matter what is involved. If you are submitting by e-mail, the word "resume" MUST appear in the subject line of your message, and the first ten characters of the resume text must begin: @@@@@@@@@@. Most important, if you are submitting by e-mail, the resume must be the main body of the text. Copy and paste your word processing document into the e-mail. Scanning programs do not open attachments to the e-mail message.

If you are submitting by fax, adjust the machine so that it transmits in the finest resolution.

If you are sending by mail, use a large envelope, and mail it without folding, bending, or otherwise marring the surface (no staples, paper clips, etc.).

In any case, prepare your resume for presentation on a white background, standard letter-size paper (8-1/2" X 11") and without the graphic features that help to provide emphasis (italics, underlining, shadows, or reverses). What you want to highlight should be done in bold face, using small capital letters, and suitable for continuous reading (no columns, for example). Similarly, limit the graphic features that can add flair to a printed resume (no horizontal or vertical lines, no boxes, minimize use of bullets, and no cute symbols).

Resume scanning programs differ about the size of type that they are programmed to read. Some start as small as 10-point; others read no smaller than 11-point. Resume scanning programs usually specify a range between 10-point and 14-point, but will vary with the type style. If your resume is done in Times New Roman (a common computer typeface) it should be no smaller than 11-point. A larger typeface (Helvetica, Arial, and Courier) is safer in the 10-point size. Where you have a choice, scanning programs appear to favor sans serif type (Arial rather than New Times Roman). Do not run letters together, regardless of size or type style.

Most important, standard resume scanning programs read standard line spacing (single or double-space). We have all drafted resumes that run two or three lines over a standard page. Many word processing programs have features (WordPerfect calls it "Make It Fit") that enable the computer to shrink the runoff to fit onto one page. DO NOT USE THESE FEATURES FOR A SCANNABLE PROGRAM.

These are the features that you need to keep in mind as you draft your resume. Unique programs will vary these instructions in some details. The only rules that apply are the ones that are specified by the agency or organization that has advertised the position. They have the job to offer; you have to play by their rules to compete at all. That is the first step to success.

(2) Adapt your presentation.

Resume scanning programs look for different features than standard written formats. Undoubtedly, computer programmers analyzed thousands of resumes, with the benefit of human resource management professionals and subject matter experts, and decided upon criteria that they would emphasize in assessing the resumes. Consider carefully what has changed.

Effective written resumes stress active verbs that impart a dynamic character to the applicant. Resume scanning programs tend to seek nouns that identify skills.

Written resumes attempt to provide additional details that make a difference, often using adjectives, adverbs, or other modifiers to grab the reader's attention. The computer seeks only terms that reflect skills identified in the resume (to match them against a vacancy announcement). Emphasize substance and avoid flair in writing for a computer scanning program.

The Resumix program used by the Department of Defense has a limit of eighty skills that it will record for any one resume. In writing such a resume, it is important to put your skills up front in as concise a manner as possible.

The DoD program encourages students to submit one-page resumes, and will not read anything beyond the third page for any applicant. Therefore, your skills summary opening of the resume and the duties associated with the first position that you describe should include the major portion of the skills that you will present in the resume.

The DoD database restricts applicants to one resume. Although applicants want to be considered for more than one job, the one-resume criteria requires that you provide the most extensive list of your qualifications, then apply for the positions that best fit the skills that score on your resume.

Do not discard the written resume targeted to a specific job. When you are called for an interview, you may still present the selecting official with a revised version of the resume that takes advantage of the active verbs and stylistic graphics.

(3) Pointers for presentation.

Develop a strong summary of skills for your initial section of text. Knowing the skill requirements for the positions that you desire will help in identifying the skills that you will want to include in this summary, but don't omit key qualifications. If you are an engineer, attorney, accountant, air traffic controller, or other specialty that can be hired anywhere from GS-5 to GS-15, get the primary qualification in the skills summary. You need to be an engineer before you can be considered for a supervisory engineering position. Get the essentials into the resume as directly as possible.

It is important to read several vacancy announcements for the variety of skills that agencies seek in filling positions similar to the ones that you want. If you are seeking a position at the GS-13 level or above, expect that some supervisory experience will be desired in addition to basic technical knowledge. At senior levels, written and oral communications skills are expected among applicants who seek to represent the agency at public meetings. Get the important details for your position into position to be recognized by the scanner as early as possible.

Position titles in federal agencies can frequently hide more than they reflect about your skills. Were you a "special assistant," "policy analyst," "management analyst," or "special projects director"? If so, modify the title to reflect the actual skills that you used in performing it. A Management Analyst (Accounting) probably did something different from a Management Analyst (Strategic Planning), or (Information Systems) or (Human Resources). Don't be tied to an old title. Describe your skills to qualify for the next position.

(4)   Skills Summary: A Comparison.

The following descriptions reflect the same person in the same position. Where the paper presentation relies heavily on active verbs to describe duties and responsibilities, the Scannable Resume presentation focuses on the skill areas and uses more nouns and fewer verbs. The qualifications have not changed; they have been targeted to the scanner's reading program. The position applied for is International Aviation Operations Specialist, GS-0301-13/14

Sample 1

Paper Resume Presentation:

Responsible for planning and developing policies and activities related to the FAA's international program; analyzing data; and conducting studies which support those policies and activities; organizing, executing, and managing activities; implementing the FAA's international policies and programs; and supporting the overall activities of the Division and office.

Scannable Resume Presentation:

Policy planner with experience in international air traffic control, airport and airways security, and aviation facilities management. Researcher who wrote reports and delivered media presentations on aviation safety and airport security topics in Asian nations and major American markets. Developed aviation operations reports to assist international negotiations and public affairs events.

Sample 2

Paper Resume Presentation:

Program Management - Organized major international meetings on air traffic control and safety initiatives leading to effective operational agreements.

Aviation Technical / Operational Support Programs - Negotiated air traffic control protocols and international agreements addressing airport security and aviation technology improvements.

Coordination with Internal-External Organizations - Coordinated international meetings on aviation technology and law enforcement. Gained support of other nations and other government agencies for major enhancements to programs.

Written Communications - Published articles addressing aviation technology and security innovations.

Oral Communications - Organized and chaired international aviation meetings. Conducted successful media presentations to gain public support for aviation technical conferences.

Scannable Resume Presentation:

Program Management, Negotiations, Internal-External Communications, International Relations, Writing Published Articles, Media Representative, Meeting Chair

International Aviation, International Air Traffic Control Agreements, International Aviation Meeting Planning, Air Traffic Control Protocols, Air Traffic Safety and Security Innovations, Airport Security, Aviation Technology Improvements, Aviation Technology Law Enforcement

Sample Resume - Text Format for Scanning

@@@@@@@@@
ROBERTA E. SPENCER
345-87-6540

124 3rd Street, NE
Washington, DC 20002

Home telephone no.: (202) 567-8910
Work Telephone no.: (202) 267-9976
E-mail Address: rspencer@ari.net

Lowest Grade Acceptable: GS-12

SKILLS SUMMARY:

Program Management, Negotiations, Internal-External Communications, International Relations, Writing Published Articles, Media Representative, Meeting Chair

International Aviation, International Air Traffic Control Agreements, International Aviation Meeting Planning, Air Traffic Control Protocols, Air Traffic Safety and Security Innovations, Airport Security, Aviation Technology Improvements, Aviation Technology Law Enforcement

RECENT ACCOMPLISHMENTS:

Facilitated international meetings of Chinese, Filipino, Indian, and Pakistani media briefings after negotiations of air traffic control protocols for Pacific Ocean flights. Prepared briefing materials and agendas, organized presentations, and ensured complete media access to technical officials. Presentations resulted in major international coverage for innovative technologies in air commerce.

Completed developmental assignment with U.S. Customs Service to publicize strengthened enforcement of smuggling laws with regard to major Asian nations. Coordinated presentations for international meetings involving Malaysian, Pakistani, and Filipino governments and presenting resolution of complex international negotiations.

Published articles in FAA World describing agency perspective on success of international negotiations. Reported advances in air traffic control technology, new agreement with the Peoples' Republic of China for maintenance of aircraft consistent with FAA standards, and new international smuggling accord.

WORK EXPERIENCE:

Oct. 1993 to present; 40 hours per week; **Deputy Public Affairs Officer**, GS-0301-12/4; promoted to GS-12 October 1993; Federal Aviation Agency, 800 Independence Avenue, SW, Washington, DC 20591; supervisor: Roger Sperrin (202) 267-9975.

Represent FAA Headquarters before general media in the absence of the Public Affairs Officer. Coordinated seven-person branch providing public information about the agency's mission, policies, and operations to ensure timely and responsive presentation of sensitive issues of aviation policy and technology. Earned recognition from print and electronic media for professionalism of briefings and quick responses to technical topics.

Managed month-long detail in FAA's Los Angeles Public Affairs Office to provide major market coverage of sensitive issues involving U.S. agencies and Asian-Pacific nations. Achieved substantial public awareness of impact of new trade agreements on international transportation systems.

Oct. 1991-1993; 40 hours per week; **FAA Aviation Education Program Manager**, GS-1035-11/12; Federal Aviation Administration, 800 Independence Avenue, SW, Washington, DC 20591; Supervisor: William Leytle (202) 267-8388.

Edited weekly employee newsletter electronically disseminated to 2,735 Washington-area FAA employees. Established systematic procedures to solicit reader input and produce a cost-effective product that kept employees knowledgeable about agency issues and programs. Innovations in on-line production technology cut distribution time by one-third while realizing 20 percent cost savings.

Promoted and encouraged partnerships with businesses, education, and government organizations involving aviation activities. Enhanced development of a multi-agency commitment to the aviation education program that reached several thousand students each year. New pilot licensing in Headquarters region increased 7 percent annually during this program.

Devised and implemented components and timelines for strengthened general aviation safety concepts in FAA's Aviation Education program. Campaign cited by AOPA for reducing general aviation accident rate during 1993.

Conducted investigative interviews with employees and members of the media to provide technical background related to revised air traffic control procedures resulting from new airport radar systems at metropolitan Washington airports.

Oct. 1988 - 1991; 40 hours per week; **Assistant Command Historian,** GS-0301-9; Department of Defense, Pacific Air Command, The Pentagon, Washington, DC 20330; Supervisor: Rod Serling (202) 737-8637

Coordinated three-member team conducting interviews with military leaders at Air Force Bases for annual historical records maintained under classified conditions. These histories averaged 800 pages in length with an equal number of pages of supporting documents. Secured and monitored publication contracts for multi-volume editions.

Designed and managed construction of two foyer exhibits for Command Headquarters. Identified key command achievements over a fifty year period; researched print and photo archives to ensure accuracy and attractiveness of presentation. Exhibits averaged 50 square-feet and included historical information on the military in Hawaii in a compatible environment with local wildlife displays.

Organized 50th anniversary reunion of more than 100 veterans from the 11th Air Force who fought in Hawaii during World War II. The event included three days of activities on Pearl Harbor Naval Station and highlighted a 45-minute video featuring many of the attendees in vintage film footage. Arranged lodging, meals, and transportation, and conducted exit interviews with 80 percent of participants before departure. Convention cited by Air Force Association Historical Society.

Sept. 1985 - Sept. 1988; 40 hours per week; **Research Historian**; GS-0301-9; Hawaii Naval Air Station, Honolulu, HI; Supervisor: Mr. John Clayton (808) 546-7785

Reviewed development and implementation of air transportation systems supporting Allied Pacific operations during World War II. Historical research developed full documentation of aircraft, airport, and airway support technologies and procedures used to integrate multinational air, sea, and land forces.

Defined resource requirements to support development of oral history and film presentations to support expansion of Base history project. Supported production of video material from Army and Navy Archives.

Published more than four significant historical articles per year based on research. Coordinated meetings of local historical association and negotiated command support for multi-media presentations.

EDUCATION:
Bachelor of Arts, Major: Speech & Communications, University of California-Los Angeles, CA, 1971.

PROFESSIONAL TRAINING:

Aviation Executive Leadership Program, U.S.D.A. Graduate School, 60 days, 1995-1996. Assistant to FAA's International Liaison Officer. Planned and coordinated multi-national meetings. Developed protocols to shift air traffic control technology to cover Pacific Ocean routes. Coordinated media presence in three-day international meetings. Secured substantial favorable coverage for the U.S. government and the agency.

Assisted the Resident Agent-in-Charge with the U.S. Customs Office for 30 days. Managed public affairs for international smuggling conference, providing important coverage for new international law enforcement protocols governing movement of passengers and freight. Supported operation through media expertise and technical familiarity with airspace system operations.

Training Courses:
Air Traffic Control History, 1994
Managing Public Communication, FAA Center for Management Development, 1993
Seven Habits of Highly Effective People, 1994
The Quality Advantage (Management), 1994
Management Skills for Non-Supervisors, 1994
Investment in Excellence (Management), 1994
Public Involvement Training, 1991
Communications Training Workshop, 1989
Constructive Communications, 1988

PUBLICATIONS:
Co-author, "Woman & Minorities in Aviation in Hawaii," Hawaii Office of Education, 1994
"Aviation Progress in the Pacific," FAA World, October 1995
"Safety Basics for the Novice Pilot," Aviation Education News, Fall 1993
Our Hawaii, marketing book used worldwide by private corporation in Hawaii, 1988
The Air War in the Pacific, (Honolulu, Air Force Historical Association), 1987

HONORS & AWARDS:
Outstanding Performance Ratings seven consecutive years, 1989 - 1995
National Award for Excellence in Aerospace Education from Civil Air Patrol (Brewer Award), 1995
FAA Employee of the Year Award (Category III, GS-12 and above), 1993
Chuck Yeager Regional Award for Excellence in Aerospace Education from Civil Air Patrol, 1992
International Film Festival Award (for production of educational film), 1979

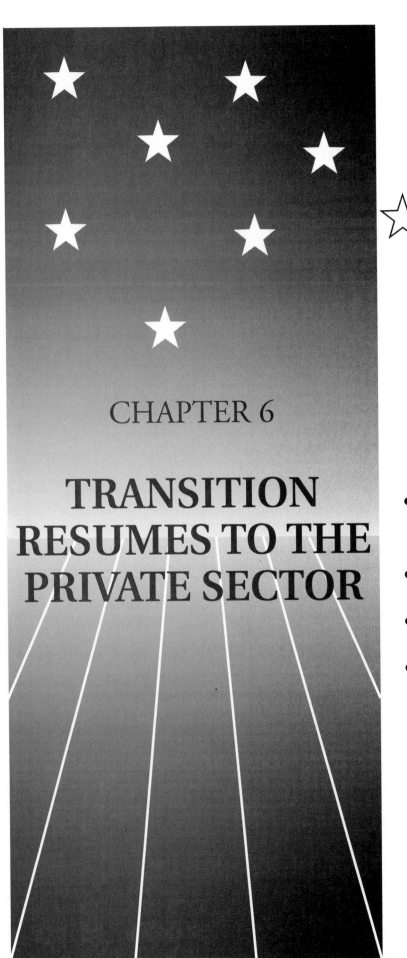

CHAPTER 6

TRANSITION RESUMES TO THE PRIVATE SECTOR

- Skills Transition into Private Sector

- Accomplishments

- Quality

- Industry Language

Transition Resumes
to the Private Sector

Now that federal agencies are accepting resumes, it should be relatively easy to make the transition from a resume submitted as an application for a federal position to a resume that should provide a potential employer in the private sector with the information necessary to evaluate your application. However, where federal resumes generally run at least three pages for seasoned people, most companies expect applicants to convey the relevant information on no more than two pages.

This exercise will work with the resume of Ronald B. Auguson, a supervisory criminal investigator who has spent most of his (entirely fictional) career in the Office of the Inspector General in the U.S. Department of Agriculture. He has fifteen years' experience in federal agencies, but this exercise has him working within the Federal Employees Retirement System. He has the advantage of portability associated with primary retirement benefits, and wants to consider private options. He might still use the federal resume if an appropriate promotional opportunity appeared, but he wants to explore options in the private sector.

Where to Start?

Let's take some obvious steps in disposing of information that is not necessary for a private employer (especially if it is information that could place you at a disadvantage).

Taking it from the top, first delete the compliance details. Private sector employers don't need Social Security numbers on a resume. They don't need to know your citizenship status before making a job offer, and most have little -- if any -- use for information about your veteran's status. If your military experience is recent, or has contributed significantly to your employment skills, you might approach your resume differently. Auguson's military experience, however, predates his college education and all relevant professional experience.

Next, proceed through each of the position descriptions, and delete any reference to salary, a supervisor's name or telephone number. Zip codes are really important if you are mailing the resume. An employer who sees that you remember the zip code of a job that you held ten years ago might wonder if you have nothing better to do with your memory. If your high school graduation is more than five years old, or you have completed a college degree, drop any reference to high school. Deleting these details is important to you, at minimum because they consume space without conveying information that you want the employer to have.

It is especially important to dispose of salary information. Most employment counselors encourage applicants to focus on the position first, then negotiate salary later. The federal resume gets these details on the table up front. From the applicant's perspective, this could provide several disadvantages in considering a transition. Perhaps the applicant will be eligible for a pension -- not needing a comparable income, but the information might convey different expectations. A federal salary might seem more than a small employer could afford. The federal resume can erect obstacles to transition by conveying this information before negotiations get started.

What is Your Objective?

The federal resume encourages applicants to identify the specific position or job classification series for which they wish to be considered. Such a limited objective should not appear in a private sector resume. Even if you have a definite next position in mind (and Mr. Auguson does) it should be conveyed as part of the overall "Profile" or "Qualifications Summary" included on the resume.

The focus is different. This introductory profile should provide a quick summary of your resume that prepares the reader for the details that will follow. It should answer, concisely, the introductory question to so many job interviews: "Tell me about yourself." As reflected on the revised resume, the answer provided can be forward-looking, indicating the range of career options that the applicant would consider a good fit for previous experiences. Unlike the federal sector, private employers rarely have "career ladders" associated with particular employment classification series.

Accomplishments

Your successes in a federal career commonly incorporate skills that should have some counterpart in the private sector. The critical concern in developing a transition resume is to make certain that the accomplishments are expressed in terms that appeal to potential private employers' needs. Private employers need to understand your ability to add value to their company, and accomplishments, or related job descriptions, should be revised to describe, in as much detail as appropriate, the strengths that an applicant brings to the position.

Most employers do not have "inspectors general" or "investigators" on their payrolls. They all have operational security concerns, however. All private organizations feel vulnerable to corporate espionage, have basic personnel and physical security requirements, and need people who have good experience supervising others and conducting basic employment skills training for new employees. The critical concern, in revising a federal resume for a private sector transition, is to identify those skill needs and address them in describing your qualifications.

As with any resume, the important dimension remains the quality of information that you can convey about yourself that is relevant to the kinds of jobs that you want. Private employers don't need to deal with federal procedures (in most cases) so emphasize your skills, the results that you achieved, and highlight the role that your skills played in achieving the results. If you have had responsibility that affects an industry in which you would like to work, demonstrate your knowledge of that industry.

Other Sections of the Resume

Additional information is useful, but it should be information that demonstrates abilities that private sector employers need. Many federal investigators have the ability to secure and execute a search warrant; private employers can't apply for them. At the same time, few private investigators have experience using major investigative data bases (for example, the National Crime Information Center) and familiarity with such sources of information might usefully be included on some resumes. Naturally, additional credentials such as computer skills, foreign languages, publications, speaking experience, honors, awards, and other indications of public recognition can be included usefully.

Formal training (other than colleges or professional degrees) can be an asset if it demonstrably contributes to skills that you will use during a transition, or if it confirms the basic professional credentials of your career. An investigator should be able to document having completed a law enforcement training course in investigative techniques. Only rarely, however, would an investigator want to list, for example, each of the weapons on which certification has been obtained in a twenty-year career. The test is always relevance to the jobs being pursued.

Generally, if information is more than ten years old, and not a significant factor in confirming present skills, omit it. Some information might be sensitive. Mr. Auguson, for example, is a veteran who completed six years of military service before entering college. He has additional work experience between his Air Force days and gaining a position in the Office of Personnel Management. His federal resume helps to confirm his age by informing the reader of a high school diploma in 1964. If he would prefer that a prospective employer not know from the start that he is more than 50, omitting the military experience and listing only the date of college graduation leaves a different impression of his age. If his Air Force experience had been with the military police, it might broaden his relevant experience and deserve inclusion. If he was a flight mechanic, it is irrelevant to the skills that he is attempting to market now.

Other information requires a set of judgment calls on the part of the person writing the resume. For some positions (private as well as public sector), a security clearance is required. If he wanted to apply for a position handling security for a nuclear power plant, this credential should be listed.

Our Revision

We have revised Mr. Auguson's presentation to emphasize his skills, but there is no substitute for research linked to your own transition plans. Read the employment advertising in your professional journals and focus on the skills that employers say that they want. Talk about your career transition interests with friends in companies that perform similar activities. Call some of your friends who recently left your agency or office, and ask them, "What is it that you brought from your federal experience that has been most useful in your new job?" Let their answers guide your description of your transition resume, up to a point.

That point, of course, needs to center on what you want to do. Based on Ronald Auguson's experience, we have rewritten his resume to explore opportunities to help agricultural employers limit their vulnerability to violations of federal laws. The resume might be revised to explore opportunities to offer consulting services to state governments in avoiding Food Stamp fraud, or to assist agricultural producers in protecting their patented food processing systems. Remember, a resume is your personal marketing tool. No matter what it says, the test of its effectiveness is your ability to use it to gain access to the employers who will want you.

Sample Federal Resume

RONALD B. AUGUSON
3456 Tenleytown Road
Silver Spring, Maryland 20910

Home: (301) 779-5328

Office: (202) 208-7654

Citizenship: United States
Veterans' Status: U.S. Navy, (June, 1961 - August, 1964)

Social Security Number: 925-24-5748
Five point preference eligible

OBJECTIVE   Supervisory Criminal Investigator, GS-1811-15
(USDA Announcement 97-23)

PROFILE

Experienced criminal investigator with exceptional record resolving criminal, civil, and administrative matters affecting federal agencies. Fifteen years with Office of the Inspector General, U.S. Department of Agriculture, successfully coordinating teams conducting complex, multi-agency investigations. Previous experience includes more than two years of uniformed law enforcement.

SIGNIFICANT ACCOMPLISHMENTS

♦   Earned Superior and Distinguished Inspector General Awards for contributions to successful public corruption investigations and prosecutions in North Carolina and Alabama. Dedicated thirty months investigation to secure convictions of more than twenty senior officials and employees in a pioneering tobacco pricing corruption case. Success figured prominently in the agency's move to full law enforcement status under the U.S. Marshal's deputation program.

♦   Played a leading role in the agency's development as a law enforcement organization Expanded scope and quality of Southeastern Division's investigations program by opening field offices in Raleigh, NC, Birmingham, AL, and Tallahassee, FL. Introduced successful use of portable computers to assist field investigations. Regularly provided recommendations to senior officials for handling complex investigations and prosecutions in a customer-driven environment.

♦   Strengthened Eastern Division investigative program through intensive on-the-job training of junior investigators. Provided strong "shirtsleeve" supervision to audit-investigations teams and task forces and enhanced reliance on administrative subpoenas and grand juries to increase civil, administrative and criminal actions. Conducted, coordinated, or supervised investigations of public corruption in tobacco and cotton pricing and grading scandals, civil and criminal contract fraud, environmental crimes, and congressional, administrative, and employee misconduct issues.

WORK EXPERIENCE

Assistant Special Agent-In-Charge   September, 1991 - Present
OFFICE OF THE INSPECTOR GENERAL/EASTERN DIVISION INVESTIGATIONS
U.S. DEPARTMENT OF AGRICULTURE   Washington, DC 20245
Starting Grade: GM-14   Current Grade: GM-14
Supervisor: Oswald T. Zetterman (202) 462-3452   Current supervisor may be contacted

Lead operations of a 15-member investigative team conducting civil, administrative, and criminal investigations to combat waste, fraud, and abuse affecting federal resources. Organize and coordinate investigations within the eastern U.S. and major crop, Food Stamp, and related prosecutions within the Department. Coordinate complex investigations with other federal agencies and prosecutors. Manage daily office operations, monitoring cases in progress and redirecting investigations through ongoing discussions and systematic analysis of agents' reports. Conduct effective training for investigations staff to ensure full professional advancement opportunities for agents.

PREVIOUS EXPERIENCE

Special Agent   February, 1988 - August, 1991
OFFICE OF THE INSPECTOR GENERAL/NORTHERN REGION INVESTIGATIONS
U.S. DEPARTMENT OF AGRICULTURE   Minneapolis, MN 55413
Starting Grade: GS-12   Ending Grade: GS-13
Supervisor: Richard Kimball (612) 345-5532

Conducted major public corruption, embezzlement, and fraud investigations in Iowa, Wisconsin, and Minnesota leading to the indictment, arrest, and conviction and plea agreements of two dozen farmers, agricultural lobbyists, and public officials. Served as senior agent for one to three field agents in multiple investigations. Demonstrated effectiveness of laptop computers in supporting field investigations through processing evidence and communicating with Department of Justice. Secured and executed search warrants of lobbying offices seeking financial records to support prosecution. Earned Department Inspector General Awards for successful investigations and convictions.

Special Agent   April, 1986 - January, 1988
OFFICE OF THE INSPECTOR GENERAL/SOUTHERN REGION INVESTIGATIONS
U.S. DEPARTMENT OF AGRICULTURE   Atlanta, GA 33567
Starting Grade: GS-12   Ending Grade: GS-12
Supervisor: Walter Allistone (404) 341-9225

Secured more than 20 criminal actions or cases accepted for prosecution after investigations. Coordinated major investigations with other federal agencies, including the FBI, Department of Labor, and Department of the Interior investigative units. Secured convictions of federal, State, and corporate officials for violations of the Mann Act, the Agricultural Resources Conservation Act, price fixing, crop assessment fraud, and theft of government property. Opened field office, and demonstrated effectiveness of field offices, leading to replication in other cities.

Special Agent   July, 1983 - March, 1986
OFFICE OF THE INSPECTOR GENERAL/SOUTHERN REGION INVESTIGATIONS
U.S. DEPARTMENT OF AGRICULTURE   New Orleans, LA
Starting Grade: GS-7   Ending Grade: GS-12
Supervisor: Mark Thomas (202) 267-3954

Conducted criminal and administrative investigations for referral to U.S. Attorneys of jurisdiction in Southern U.S. Analyzed information gathered, assessed evidence and witnesses, and wrote reports to describe findings in support of further investigation and prosecution. Coordinated efforts with other federal, state, and local law enforcement agencies. Secured Food Stamp fraud convictions and opened leads in major investigation of rice shipping fraud.

Investigator   March, 1980 - July, 1983
U.S. OFFICE OF PERSONNEL MANAGEMENT   Butte, MT 89976
Starting Grade: GS-5   Ending Grade: GS-7
Supervisor: Jack Spratt (No longer with agency)

Conducted background investigations to assess federal employees and applicants for positions with federal agencies and contractors. Assessed information that might raise questions related to the subjects suitability for federal employment and/or to evaluate information related to security. Recognized for superior investigations and reports.

HONORS AND AWARDS

Quality Step Increase	1995
Outstanding Performance Ratings	Consistently since 1988
Inspector General's Superior Service Award	1990
Inspector General's Distinguished Service Award	1989
Special Achievement Award	1988
Distinguished Graduate, Criminal Investigations School	1984

EDUCATION

MA	**Western Carolina University**	*Criminal Justice*	January, 1972
	Cullowhee, North Carolina 29978		
BS	**James Madison University**	*Sociology*	May, 1969
	Harrisonburg, Virginia 25350		
	General Beedle State University	*Liberal Arts*	Sept., 1965 - May, 1966
	Pierre, South Dakota 76543		
	Sacred Heart High School		Graduated, 1964
	Dubuque, Iowa 65449		

PROFESSIONAL TRAINING

Federal Law Enforcement Training Center	Washington, DC	Criminal Investigations	1984
Federal Law Enforcement Training Center	San Francisco, CA	Procurement Fraud	1983
Federal Law Enforcement Training Center	Washington, DC	Law Enforcement/ Park Rangers	1976

Our Revision - Private Sector Resume

RONALD B. AUGUSON
3456 Tenleytown Road
Silver Spring, Maryland 20910

Home: (301) 779-5328   Office: (202) 462-3450

PROFILE

Experienced criminal investigator with exceptional record resolving criminal, civil, and administrative matters affecting agricultural firms. Successfully coordinated conduct of complex, multi-agency investigations. Extensive knowledge of financial data and fraud investigation techniques. Seeking opportunity to develop company programs to ensure compliance with federal laws and regulations affecting agricultural operations.

SIGNIFICANT ACCOMPLISHMENTS

◆ Earned Superior and Distinguished Inspector General Awards for contributions to successful public corruption investigations and prosecutions in North Carolina and Alabama. Dedicated thirty month investigation to secure convictions of more than twenty senior officials and employees in a pioneering tobacco pricing corruption case. Developed thorough knowledge of tobacco marketing practices to identify vulnerabilities and assist detection of illegal fund uses.

◆ Coordinated major operations supporting Immigration and Naturalization Service crackdown on employment of illegal aliens in food packing businesses. Secured administrative and criminal penalties against more than 125 firms, resulting in deportation of more than 500 aliens with felony convictions. Coordinated development of programs with North Carolina, South Carolina, Georgia and Alabama employment divisions to provide eligible applicants for positions.

◆ Strengthened Eastern Division investigative program through intensive on-the-job training of junior investigators. Provided strong "shirtsleeve" supervision to audit-investigations teams and task forces to increase civil and criminal actions. Conducted, coordinated, or supervised investigations of corruption in tobacco and cotton pricing scandals. Secured civil and criminal convictions for contract fraud, environmental crimes, and illegal financial transactions.

RECENT EXPERIENCE

Assistant Special Agent-In-Charge   September, 1991 - **Present**
OFFICE OF THE INSPECTOR GENERAL/EASTERN DIVISION INVESTIGATIONS
U.S. DEPARTMENT OF AGRICULTURE   Washington, DC

Lead operations of a 15-member investigative team conducting civil, administrative, and criminal investigations to combat waste, fraud, and abuse of federal resources. Organize and coordinate investigations involving major crop, Food Stamp, and fraud prosecutions. Monitor cases in progress and redirect investigations through systematic analysis of agents' reports. Initiated Department participation in federal data bases for tracing criminal suspects and checking backgrounds.

Ronald B. Auguson   **Page 2**

Special Agent   February, 1988 - August, 1991
OFFICE OF THE INSPECTOR GENERAL/NORTHERN REGION INVESTIGATIONS
U.S. DEPARTMENT OF AGRICULTURE   Minneapolis, MN
Conducted major corruption, embezzlement, and fraud investigations in Iowa, Wisconsin, and Minnesota. Secured indictment, arrest, and conviction or plea agreements of twenty-four farmers, lobbyists, and public officials. Demonstrated effectiveness of laptop computers in supporting field investigations through processing evidence and communicating with Department of Justice. Secured and executed search warrants of lobbying offices seeking financial records to support prosecution.

PREVIOUS EXPERIENCE

Special Agent   April, 1986 - January, 1988
OFFICE OF THE INSPECTOR GENERAL/SOUTHERN REGION INVESTIGATIONS
U.S. DEPARTMENT OF AGRICULTURE   Atlanta, GA
Secured more than 20 criminal actions or cases accepted for prosecution after investigations. Coordinated major investigations with other federal agencies, including the FBI, Department of Labor, and Department of the Interior investigative units. Secured convictions of federal, state, and corporate officials for violations of the Pure Food and Drug Act, price fixing, crop assessment fraud, and theft of government property.

Special Agent   July, 1983 - March, 1986
OFFICE OF THE INSPECTOR GENERAL/SOUTHERN REGION INVESTIGATIONS
U.S. DEPARTMENT OF AGRICULTURE   New Orleans, LA
Conducted criminal and administrative investigations for referral to U.S. Attorneys of jurisdiction in Southern U.S. Coordinated efforts with other federal, state, and local law enforcement agencies. Secured Food Stamp fraud convictions and opened leads in major investigation of rice shipping fraud.

Investigator   March, 1980 - July, 1983
U.S. OFFICE OF PERSONNEL MANAGEMENT   Butte, MT
Conducted background investigations to assess federal employees and applicants for positions with federal agencies and contractors.

COMPUTER SKILLS
Proficient using NCIC, Alien Eligibility Systems, and major financial transaction systems. Effective with standard word processing and data base management software.

HONORS AND AWARDS
Outstanding Performance Ratings   Consistently since 1988
Inspector General's Superior Service Award   1990
Inspector General's Distinguished Service Award   1989
Special Achievement Award   1988
Distinguished Graduate, Criminal Investigations School   1984

EDUCATION
MA   ***Western Carolina University***   *Criminal Justice*   January, 1972
BS   ***James Madison University***   *Sociology*   May, 1969

PROFESSIONAL TRAINING
Federal Law Enforcement Training Center   Washington, DC   Criminal Investigations   1984
Federal Law Enforcement Training Center   San Francisco, CA Procurement Fraud   1983

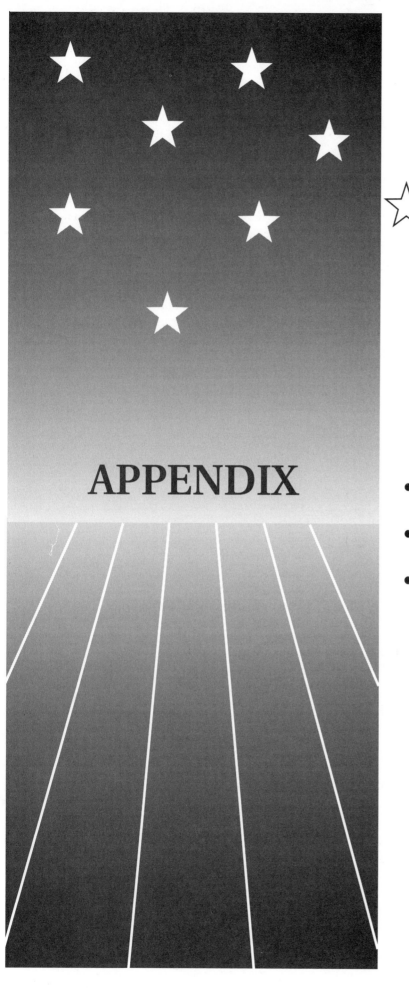

APPENDIX

- Reinvention Language

- Job Search Websites

- Resume Writing Sources

Reinvention Language

The Editor of *Reinvention Express, National Performance Review,* uses certain verbs, adverbs and adjectives to describe reinvention success stories by the federal workforce. These are the new "buzz words" for writing federal job descriptions, projects and accomplishments. Federal agencies that are involved in the "reinvention process" include this language in their job announcements, mission statements, and in their daily operations management. Be sure to include them in your Federal Resume, KSAs, ECQs and cover letter. Read the reinvention stories by visiting the Newsroom at http://www.npr.gov.

VERBS (Action Words)
(Words in parentheses show sample verb usage)

Achieve (goals)
Adapt
Adopt
Applauded
Approach (to achieving)
Build
Challenge
Change (the way to do business)
Charge (take charge)
Collaborate
Combine (funds)
Concentrate
Conduct (rules)
Consolidate (programs)
Cooperate (with)
Correct (violations)
Cost-saving (ways or devices)
Create
Cut (development time)
Cut (red tape)
Cutting (edge)
Demonstrate
Design
Detect
Develop (software)
Eliminate
Empower
Evaluate (responses)
Exhibit (excellence)
Extend (market incentives)
Focus (of the project)
Focus on
Form (labor-management partnerships)
Foster (innovations)

High quality standards uphold
Identify (priorities and standards)
Implement
Improve
Improve (customer service)
Incorporate (findings)
Initiate
Interact
Jeopardize
Joined (forces)
Move (workers to the front)
Moving toward
Negotiate
Quick
React
Reduce (overall)
Reengineer
Reinvent (processes)
Relieve (the paperwork burden)
Remove (stumbling blocks)
Replace
Respond (to customers)
Restructure (work goals)
Restructuring (agency)
Review
Reward
Set (specific goals)
Shrink
Step up (service campaign)
Streamline
Stress (common sense)
Strive
Supervise
Transform
Waive (any statutory requirements)
Work together

ADVERBS

(Words to describe verbs)
(Verbs in parenthesis)

Aggressively (demonstrated)
Ambitiously (studied to improve)
Brilliantly (planning)
Carefully (planned)
Completely (finished the project)
Continuously (followed up)
Cooperatively (worked together)
Creatively (moved ahead)
Effectively (improved)
Efficiently (handled)
Enthusiastically (supported)
Helpfully (worked with teammates)
Innovatively (planned)
Meticulously (arranged)
Painstakingly (followed through)
Patiently (figuring)
Quickly (followed up)
Responsibly (arranged meetings)
Speedily (moved ahead)
Successfully (measured)
Systematically (projected)
Tentatively (settled on plans)
Timely (planning for projects)
Timely (writing)

NOUNS

(Names of persons or things)

Alternative systems
An approach (to problems)
Challenge
Common practice
Common sense
Comprehensive review
Creative team
Customer service plan
Cut (of the budget)
Effective measurement techniques
Elimination (of the problem)
Flexibility
Goals of achieving
Goals of improving
Implementation
Increased responsiveness
Initiatives
Innovation
Installed program
Integrated team
Interagency team
Labor-Management partnerships
Legislative proposals
Level of service
Measurement
New ways to conduct business
Overall results
Paperwork burden
Partnership
Partnership with industry
Partnerships with coworkers
Performance measurement
Performance measurement system
Pledges of service
Presidential Directives
Priority
Process of continuous improvement
Program to avoid delays
Public contacts
Reaction
Red tape
Reforms we implement
Regulations
Regulatory burden
Regulatory philosophy
Results
Rewarding results
Service campaign
Shrinking budget
Significant contribution
Solutions (to problems)
Sophisticated analyses
Standards
Standards (in customer service report)
Status of the claim
Status report
Stumbling blocks
Successful methods
System that is successful
Teams (that cooperate)
Timely data
Who implement effectively

ADJECTIVES

(Descriptive words)

Aggressive
Avoiding delays
Budget-conscious
Community spirited
Comprehensive
Conscious improvement
Continuously improve
Cost-saving
Creative
Effective
Efficient
Empowered (to make decisions)
Expensive delays
Fast moving
Fast-paced
Flexible
Hands-on
Improved
Innovative
Integrated (system)
Interagency
Obsolete (regulations)
Out-of-date
Quick
Reengineered
Regulatory
Replaced
Rewording
Reworking
Sophisticated
Successful
Sweeping (legislation)
The most serious
Timely (data)
Transformed
Underfunded
User-friendly

Recommended Federal and Private Industry Websites

Federal Government Jobs and Employment Information
USAJOBS - United States Office of Personnel Management – Federal job openings are easy to access at this site. http://www.usajobs.opm.gov/

Government Jobs Career Center – Dennis Damp's outstanding government/career site. http://members.aol.com/govjobs/index.htm (Government Jobs)

Planning Your Future - The Federal Employee's Survival Guide – Many resources here for federal job-seekers. http://safetynet.doleta.gov/

The National Performance Review – *If you want to be inspired to write a great reinvention federal resume, check out the reinvention stories here before writing.* http://www.npr.gov/

Books & Publications on Federal Employment:
The Federal Resume Guidebook & PC Disk, Kathryn K. Troutman, 242 pgs. A comprehensive guide to Federal Resume Writing, KSAs, ECQs, letters. http://www.resume-place.com/jobs

Applying for Federal Jobs, Patricia B. Wood Tips and formats for completing the new OF-612. http://www.clubfed.com/afj.html

Electronic Job Search:
The Riley Guide - *excellent* Margaret Riley's premier job search website. An invaluable resource. http://www.dbm.com/jobguide

eResumes & Resources – incredible, award-winning site by Rebecca Smith Internet Training & Electronic Resume Management http://www.eresumes.com

Scannable Resume Writing:
Resumix™, Inc., "Preparing the Ideal Scannable Resume" *Resumix™ is the software that Federal agencies are using – great tips here !* http://www.resumix.com/resume/resume-tips.html

Department of Defense Civilian Military Job Kits and Employment Info:
Job Listings & Resume Databases; Job Kits include instructions for writing scannable resumes.
Washington Headquarters Services, National Capital Region - http://www.hrsc.osd.mil/
U.S. Air Force Personnel Center - http://dpcweb.afpc.af.mil/ga1.htm
Army Civilian Personnel Online - http://cpol.army.mil/
There is no Armywide Job Kit. Each Army Region has unique procedures and corresponding job kits. Click on *Employment Opportunities*; Click on the *State* or *Region*; Open *Army Vacancy Announcements* and read the *"How to Apply"* instructions on the announcement. After Nov. 1997: open *"On-line Resume"* for a standardized resume format.

The Resume Place, Inc.
PUBLICATIONS & SERVICES

K. Troutman, The Federal Resume Guidebook & PC Disk 2.0 - $34.95

An invaluable resource, the Guidebook is the first book on writing the new Federal Resume based on the OF-510. The Guidebook (242 pages) includes samples, step-by-step instructions, chapters on KSAs, SES ECQs, covering letters, and more. Outstanding chapter on editing and converting the lengthy SF-171 job descriptions into short, concise, accomplishments-based descriptions.

New Bonus Federal Resume PC Disk 2.0 includes: Seven Federal Resume samples in Word 6.0 and Word Perfect 5.1 (College Student, Law Student, Interior Dept., Procurement Analyst, Program Manager, Realty Specialist, Scannable E-mail); Blair House Papers Review; Favorite Federal Website list; OSD Job Kit; Scannable Resume Instructions; FAQ from workshops.

Transition Center/Multiple User Disk: $150.00 (each PC). Disk is available separately for $19.95 for individual users.

K. Troutman, Reinvention Federal Resumes - $19.95

Hot off the press, this 104-page federal resume writing workbook includes 12 resume writing exercises (with space for writing), following OF-510 compliance guidelines, as well as many "reinvention" resume writing strategies. The workbook includes a complete case study of an announcement for a GS-12 federal resume, KSA set, and cover letter. The federal resume is also redesigned into a scannable format ready for e-mail into an automated federal database. The same resume is also formatted into a one-page "calling card" presentation for networking.

15% discount for 10 or more workbooks.

K. Troutman, Reinvention Resume PC Disk 1.0 - $19.95

A supplemental disk to the _Reinvention Federal Resumes_ workbook, includes five great-looking sample resumes in Word 6.0 and Word Perfect 6.1: Two 3-4 page federal resumes; one 2-page private industry resume; a 1-page "calling-card" resume; a 3-page Resumix™ resume for Washington Service Center, National Capitol Region; also the KSA and cover letter for Roberta Spencer's federal application.

Career Transition Center/Multiple User Price: $150.00 (for each PC).

K. Troutman, High School Student's Resume Writing Handbook - $9.95

First of its kind, this _School to Work Initiative_ resume writing handbook was inspired by Kathryn's three high-school teenagers. Students will learn how to market their high school experiences toward college and careers in this user-friendly, 48-page handbook.

Coming November 1997.

Federal Job Search Consulting, Critiques & Resume Writing Services

The Resume Place, Inc., Kathryn K. Troutman, President, Offices in Washington, DC and Baltimore, MD. Expert, professional consultation, writing, editing, design and word processing of targeted, concise and effective resumes.

Appointments and estimates: (410) 744-4324; Fax: (410) 744-0112.

Workshops: Federal Resumes, Scannable Resumes and KSA Writing

Outstanding interactive, PC-overhead workshops concentrating on resume writing, skills development, writing and editing a concise federal resume targeting specific positions and/or series. Workshop agenda is on The Resume Place website.

Federal Resume Writing Website: http://www.resume-place.com/jobs

The only website specializing in federal resume writing. Updated frequently with new federal resume samples and federal employment information. Bookmark this site!

The Resume Place – Order Form

Simply fill out order form and mail – OR – call (410) 744-4324 or FAX (410) 744-0112.

Quantity	Product Title	Unit Price	Total
		Subtotal	
		+5% Sales Tax MD residents	
		Shipping/ Handling	
		Total	

Purchase Order # _____

Shipping Information:

Organization Name: _____

Contact: _____

Street Address: _____

_____

City: _____ State: _____ Zip: _____

Phone: _____

Billing Information: (if different)

Organization Name: _____

Contact: _____

Street Address: _____

_____

City: _____ State: _____ Zip: _____

Phone: _____

Credit Card Orders: _____ VISA _____ MC _____ AMEX

Card #: _____ Exp. Date: _____

Signature: _____

Please copy this form if you need more lines for your order and/or for future orders!

Shipping • Handling

In the continental U.S.:
- Minimum per book: $6.00
- Multiple orders: priced per no. of books purchased. Call for amount.

Outside the continental U.S.:
- Call The Resume Place at (410) 744-4324 for an estimate of the fees.

Thank You for your order!

THE RESUME PLACE, INC.
310 Frederick Road
Baltimore, MD 21228
Phone: (410) 744-4324
Fax: (410) 744-0112
E-mail: resume@ari.net